SOUL MENDING

SOUL MENDING

Letters to Friends in Crisis

JOSEPH P. BISHOP

MOREHOUSE-BARLOW
Wilton, Conn.

Morehouse Barlow Co., Inc.
78 Danbury Road
Wilton, Connecticut 06897

Library of Congress Cataloging-in-Publication Data

Bishop, Joseph P.
Soul mending.

1. Consolation. I. Title.
BV4905.2.B49   1986   248.8'6   86-4321
ISBN 1-8192-1379-9

Printed in the United States of America

2 4 6 8 10 9 7 5 3 1

To KARL

1905-1985

Contents

I wish to express my gratitude to Stephen Wilburn, Editorial Director of Morehouse-Barlow, whose confidence and encouragement have made these letters available. There is in him a blend of competence and compassion which can only be a writer's blessing. Nor can I forget to thank Sally Mead, my secretary, whose patient deciphering of my handwriting and diagrams surpasses understanding, as well as Marilyn Nardone, whose editorial suggestions have been invaluable. Finally, I must convey my appreciation to the friends and families represented in these pages who have given me permission to publish these letters in the hope that they will be of value to others in similar crises.

Preface

These letters are written to persons I have loved for many years. Each one represents a real experience we have shared. In most instances I have changed the names and places for purposes of anonymity, but in no case have I changed the facts or the truth of the situation. The crises were real. Much of the material is taken from my journals, covering a span of forty-five years of ministry to people of all sorts and in all conditions of the soul.

For me, the richest vein of enrichment in those years was found in the gold mine of counseling and personal friendships. It is a priceless privilege to share the anguish of people who are faced with the imminence of death, the pain of grief, the hurt of betrayal and divorce, the loss of faith, the confusion of caring for a disoriented loved one in a nursing home, the shock of dealing with a son's or a daughter's preference for the same sex, the tragedy of AIDS in a son, or the ravages of alcohol and drug addiction.

In these letters I have tried to describe our experience in all these conditions, as prized friends have shared their pain and their dismay with me. The struggle for faith in the living God was central to the way in which we dealt with our anguish. In some lives we came to a resolution of the issues; in others the issues are still in the process of being resolved.

These pages reflect my love and devotion to many friends in the crises of life. When we are wounded by the disappointments of life, we often find healing when a hidden peace is awakened in us by a loving stream that comes from someone who loves us. I pray that those who read these letters may be touched by that healing stream and know from whence it comes!

SOUL MENDING

My dear Camille,

You are my friend with the wistful eyes. Last night the sky above the ocean was weird. It was one of those times when it makes you dizzy to watch the moon. Great streaks of dark clouds moved with breathtaking speed in a southwesterly direction. The moon rode on the clouds as though it were carried by huge black swans flying before a tempest. I often get the feeling when we talk about your thirst for God that your soul is like last night's sky. There is a brightness in you that illumines, but it shines behind clouds driven by winds of high intensity.

Traditional religion for you is a constraint. It threatens your freedom. Its doctrine is anathema. Too much is claimed on too little evidence. The world seems to you to have been hideously cursed by the rigidities and cruelties of religion. It is intolerable for you when you think of all the crimes that have been committed in the name of Christ. The world, in your opinion, would be a more civilized place if the claims of infallibility and the dogmatisms of all religions could be dropped into the dustbin of history.

You often say to me, "Let's grow up and be

responsible, decent, globally conscious human beings. We
don't need religion to do that for us. The burden is ours.
Let the human race become mature and stand up to our
responsibilities for one another as living beings on this
fragile island home, the earth.''

Every word you speak overflows with truth. Who can
deny the witness of history against religion? Is there any
more vicious, cruel, and threatening combination in the
human record than the linkage between dogmatic religion
and political power? The religion of the Third Reich is the
most recent and devastating illustration of the point, but it
is far from being alone.

I also embrace your call for an adult attitude toward our
problems of survival on this delicately balanced planet. I,
too, long to see us throw off the creeping, paralyzing fear
that we are helpless victims of our fate in this nuclear age.
Would to God we could be ''mature'' and stand up to our
responsibilities as you beg us to do.

However relevant these issues may be, Camille, they are
not the ones that preoccupy you and me at our present
stages of life. You are exceptionally sensitive to the wounds
we Christians continue to inflict upon the body of Christ by
our insensitivities and our self-centeredness. It surpasses
your imagination to understand how this heavenly treasure
should be so narrowly contained in an earthly vessel that
knows so little about sublime and holy adoration. You have
quoted your favorite maxim to me a hundred times, ''Every
utterance in religion which does not result in obedience is
ultimately a scandal to the Christ of justice and peace; and
every prayer that does not end in silent adoration is barely
worthy of the name of God.'' The absence of humble

obedience and holy adoration in the church and in her councils wearies you and turns you away from her nurture.

But, Camille, you need the church! You need her disciplines, her work of worship we call her liturgies, her sacraments, her honor of God's word, her symbols and signs of grace. I didn't realize how much I needed all those graces, especially the Eucharist, until I recently added the holy orders of a priest in the Episcopal church to my Presbyterian ministry of well over forty years. We both need the church, Camille, no matter what her wounds may yet be.

Thank you for reading Meister Eckhart last month. It is beyond belief that six hundred years separate us from him. He is contemporary, fresh, profound, isn't he? Do you remember the passage where he writes: "There is an agent in the soul, untouched by time and flesh, which proceeds out of the spirit and which remains forever in the spirit—in this agent, God is perpetually verdant and flowering with all the joy and glory that is in him. Here is joy so inconceivably great that no one can ever fully tell it, for in this agent the eternal Father is ceaselessly begetting his eternal Son."

Every time I see you I perceive "a flowering and a verdant joy" that emanates from your center. The mark of its authenticity is that you are wholly unconscious of the effect you have on people. I am not, by any means, the only person to see this quality in you. Events, people, flowers, trees, morning and evening light, are curiously transformed by your presence. You see things other people don't see. Small children are immediately comfortable in your presence. Cats begin to purr and rub themselves against you when you enter a house. Dogs want to be recognized and petted. I have seen strong, brusque aggressive men become

shy when you ask them the simplest question about their
welfare. You seem as much at home with people of privilege
and power as you are with the plumber who comes to fix
your toilet. You are the confidante of more women than
anyone I know. You are never hurried. Things always seem
to work out for you, no matter what you forget or how
confused you may be about a train schedule or a plane
reservation. When someone points out to you that you are
wearing one brown shoe and one black shoe, or that there is
something wrong about the combination of blouse and skirt
you have on, it only becomes an occasion of wild hilarity,
never embarrassment. There is a superabundance of
graciousness that seems inexhaustible in you. I've seen you
so weary you could scarcely walk, but you go to sleep so
quickly and you sleep so deeply that an hour seems to
restore your vitality as fully as a child's following an
afternoon nap.

Camille, I know your secret, but I'm afraid to write
about it for fear of spoiling it. The Metropolitan Museum of
Art had a dazzling display of the Tutankhamen treasures
not long ago. There was a golden necklace that fascinated
me. The skill of the workmanship was unbelievably lovely.
A glass case enclosed the necklace. I was glad, not only
because consequently it was protected, but also because if
everyone touched it, as I surely wanted to do, it would soon
have ceased to be a thing of beauty. That's the way I feel
about you. The flowering and verdant joy in you should be
left untouched as a sacred gift, which those of us who know
you and love you should protect by our silence and our
reverence.

Nevertheless, I feel compelled to say it. Camille, I know

the living Christ is the center of your being, and I don't think you realize it—or do you? I must apologize for being so direct. Every time we talk religion, we get hung up on the rigidities and inconsistencies that make religion so inimical to your spirit. You tell me about someone who has offended your innate courtesy and sensibility by asking you if you are a Christian, or about someone else who is making a fast track in your direction to get you into their conservative Bible study group.

You see, people sense that you are different, and they don't quite know what to do with you; but they want to expropriate you into their frame of reference. I know I will anger you when I tell you I have sometimes said to people, "Don't you see the Christ in her? Rejoice in it, and keep you cotton-pickin' fingers off of her."

When you were sick, I saw what a remarkable collection of the mystics you have in your bedroom. And I didn't fail to catch the worn and tattered look of your New Testament and the Prayer Book. Camille, am I right? I think you guard your spiritual life with a fierce privacy because it's too sacred to and indispensable for your existence to risk losing an ounce of its power by dissipation and talk! All those questions about the church you have thrown at me are just a screen to defend yourself from self-revelation, aren't they?

The tip-off was that tiny postscript at the end of your last letter. You wrote in small print, "Would you please become my confessor? Don't laugh. I'm serious." That P.S. is a crack in the rock of your resistance to the church.

I wish I knew how that deep, quiet radiant center of compassion and love became the wellspring of your being. You try to hide it under an astringency of comment about the church and religion's defeat of religion, but your words are soon forgotten. What remains is your silence and your presence.

Your silence is more eloquent than any words you speak. Teach me about it, won't you? I have long known the blessedness of a balance between solitude and solidarity, between aloneness and togetherness. Too much separateness feeds the demon of despair. Too much sociability starves the soul. You seem to live with that rhythm as easily as breathing, but you have an added dimension. Isn't it silence?

There is a steadfast quietness you bring to God in daily devotion until your soul becomes like a calm, unclouded night sky. Beneath the slow rhythmic breathing of your silent meditation, a work of grace is quietly mending that which the day has torn, and healing that which the noontide heat has burned.

Even in the sorrow and labor of your regular routine, a silent center is preserved. There is an awareness of the eternal in you, unspoken yet real. I sense an expectation of epiphanies! I wonder how many times in a week the Eternal is revealed to you in tragedy as well as in joy? Is your silence about these things the homage you feel toward the sacred?

How I yearn for your gift. Its manifestation would naturally be different for me, as it is for all of us. Yet I long for the mysterious completion silence brings. My experience of its depths is enough to know a fraction of its grace. My difficulty is that I defeat my desire constantly. In my daily walk I am drawn like hunting dogs to the scent. I travel in packs, my mind crowded with people, with frivolous and petty concerns, with passionate longings, with feverish activities, with a thousand secret escape routes from silence.

It seems wholly beyond my capacities to ponder the possibility that I could attain the silence I have seen in you after hard words and bitter deceptions have cut you down, or when the rude shock of betrayal has disarmed you. It is a silence of heroism as strong and brave as the courage of a soldier who refuses to leave his wounded comrade behind under enemy fire.

It is a loving silence known only to you and God! Camille, how do you do that? The day after you discovered what a prized friend had said and done to betray your friendship, how did you manage so much unaffected compassion, how did you remain lovingly silent? All you would say to me was "Love is not love if love refuses forgiveness."

Camille, you are unique in my experience. Your soul is one of the most Christ-filled souls I've ever known. Yet you will have nothing to do with the church. You see her flaws so vividly you make me tremble for God's judgment on Ecclesia; you loathe dogmatic assertions about conversion and heaven and hell; you wistfully yearn to know more and more about God, the living Lord. In spite of all that your consciousness overflows with the vibrancy of Christ, and now you ask me if I will be your confessor!

You told me once, "I was not baptized those many years ago to belong to the church but to Christ." Let's not get into that old discussion of ours about the indispensability of institutions for the perpetuation of civilized existence, Camille, because all I want to say for now is please continue to grow in the grace of Christ, and let's leave the future to take care of itself.

Your vocation, all unknown to you, is to be in Christ, not to speak of it, not to do more than you do, but to be. I have seen tears before the world's suffering and injustice; I have seen silence in you that was more holy than the silence that clothes the dead. A work of grace goes on in your consciousness season after season. In that deep quietude of yours, let it grow as roses bud and bloom, emerging from their green-cupped stems only to fill the air with their silent fragrance. Persevere, Camille, in your quiet ways, all unseen by others, maintaining your practices of solitariness and listening, leaving room for Christ to fill your conscious and unconscious being, modeling you through his grace.

Years ago, I was flying from Honduras back to New York. I was enthralled when the pilot directed us to observe the flow of the Gulf of Mexico into the Atlantic Ocean. You could see it clearly! A great flow of powerful emerald green water was sweeping into the blue of the Atlantic. An unforgettable sight.

Not long ago I was in Switzerland. My hostess and I were driving through the snow-clad Alps. At the foot of several declivities, along the edges of the fast running streams, I saw violet and white wild flowers bending their heads above the flowing waters. "How does it happen that you have spring flowers growing in February?" I asked my friend. "The Gulf Stream affects our climate in Switzerland," she said.

I thought of those green waters I had seen years previously and the thousands of miles and fathomless ocean depths between Switzerland and Mexico, and then I thought of Christ. Camille, in you I see the energy that was released into the ocean with verdant and flowering power in everything you say and do. You are permeated with Christ consciousness, and the beautiful thing is that you haven't the slighest idea of what I am talking about. It simply is, and it has grown in you with a steady increase of fruitfulness for which you disclaim any responsibility. It merely happens wherever you are. People say to me, "I just like being in the same room where she is."

Even though you have your problems with the accoutrements of religion, you are in love with the gospel figure. You honor him; you adore him; you worship him. Your being is filled with his love of you. Your consciousness is rooted and grounded in him.

The amazing thing is that you are only another example of this alteration of human consciousness that has been going on for two thousand years. There is nothing in history with which to compare it. Vishnu of the Hindus has not changed our consciousness of identity and destiny, nor has Muhammad, nor has Moses, nor has Buddha. Such an alteration in the creature's consciousness could only have come to us through an impulse of abundant power from the Creator. No man, however gifted or inspired, could have done it from his own resources. Only a God-man could have channeled such a salvation. The garden of Gethsemane was the place where the veil of eternity lifted ever so slightly. It was there that we had a fleeting glimpse of the cost of that alteration; but it happened, and it goes on happening in its living resurrected presence in people like you, Camille. Although you are oblivious of the grace that flows from you, no one who knows you has any doubt about the source of your joy. That is blessedness, Camille; it is the blessedness of holy presence.

That is something we both know a lot about. On that point you and I are in total harmony. The word we have

often used is the word "presence." For both of us, all
things are sacraments of presence. We sit before an open fire
in the library of my home. My yellow Labrador is asleep on
the floor nearby. Peggy has made a bouquet of wild
autumnal meadow flowers. They breathe their fragrance
upon the room from a table at the side of my chair. We are
silent together. A cloisonné icon of Christ the King, with
one hand holding the orb of the world and the other raised
in sovereign blessing, hangs on the wall. Beyond us is a
metal reproduction of the figure of St. Francis with a bird
perched on his shoulder. On another wall is a delicate oval
portrait of a fourteen-year-old almond-eyed girl, an ancestor
of my family, painted in the 1830s. Books surround us on all
the walls from floor to ceiling. The fire glows with the coals
of the wood it has already consumed. Sparks ignite and
engulf a new log I throw on the andirons. Between us there
is a mysterious Other One whom we both reverence beyond
the power of speech to declare.

Camille, that room overflows with presence! There is
the presence of the fire, ancient protector and mysterious
source of life. There is the presence of the field flowers,
familiar, slightly pungent, still warm with the autumn sun.
There is the presence of my dog, affectionate, quick to
respond to every move of my body, even to every thought
and mood of my spirit. There is the presence of the icon,
strange, overruling, the image of the kingdom we seek.
There is the portrait of a fresh, sober girl with her twinkly
eyes and straight hair, parted in the middle, gazing down on
our quietness. There is the presence of the pure-hearted St.
Francis with hands raised in benediction. There is your
deep, silent, serene, peace-giving presence, asking nothing,
but giving everything. And there is the presence of the

unseen but not unfelt one between us. It is the one from whom all presence flows. We are present to one another because in the silence we have made ourselves available to the Other One's presence; that one who clothes all things and all persons with presence, if only we will pause long enough to be grasped by it. That presence is none other than the stream of sanctifying grace that entered the ocean of human consciousness at "Bethlehem of Judea in the days of Herod the King."

The Benedicite is the only way I can end this letter. It praises the mystery of being as you and I would wish to do it.

Let the earth glorify the Lord,
  praise him and exalt him forever.
Glorify the Lord, O ye mountains and hills,
  and all that grows upon the earth,
  praise him and exalt him forever.
Glorify the Lord, O ye springs of water, seas, and streams,
  O ye whales and all that move in the waters.
  all ye birds of the air, glorify the Lord,
  praise him and exalt him forever.
Glorify the Lord, O ye spirits and souls of the righteous,
  praise him and exalt him forever,
You that are holy and humble of heart, glorify the Lord,
  praise him and exalt him forever.

                    With love and faith always,

                    Joseph +

Dear Ben,

We have spent so many hours together in the last twenty-five years talking about many things, but we never talk about the one thing that matters most. I have raised it gently. You have raised it jokingly.

After the deaths of beloved family members in each of our families, we have faced the issue squarely, but since we are both such emotional creatures, rational discussion at such times of stress was out of the question. On a few occasions you said, with quaking voice, "If there is nothing on the other side, then life makes no sense at all. Everything important is waste, absurd, stupid waste." I would agree. Later when I reminded you of those words, you dismissed me. "Forget it. Forget it. Let's not talk about it." And that was that.

After we were both widowers we began our habit of dining quietly together in your home once a week. I hope I do not take advantage of your kindness. It comforts me to have you say repeatedly that you loathe dining out, and I do realize we would never have such extended and personal conversation in public as we have in your home. In addition, no restaurant I know can match the meals Tommy and Della prepare and serve.

I must say I am grateful you have stopped being a real bore about drinks before dinner. I enjoy one, especially one of the kind Tommy mixes, but at last you have stopped ringing for Tommy to come and "refresh" my drink with that malicious glee of yours, adding, "Let's see how much our little minister can hold."

Sometimes, Ben, you really are impossible. When you occasionally greet me, "Well, how is our fat little parson this week?" I know it accomplishes nothing to say "Bug off, Ben." If you're in a poozily mood, nothing I say is heard anyway. There are rare evenings when you are positively possessed with malice. Nothing I say moves you from the rails of your determined hostility toward the enemy of the moment. It doesn't matter how I try to divert your attention by raising questions of personalities. You manage quickly to steer the discussion to the object of your obsessive anger. When you have directed that hostility to me, I am left with no alternative but to get up and make my excuses to leave. "Don't go away mad!" you shout after me. At that point the only response I can make is "I'll see you next week."

Naturally, one of the things that endears you to me is the way you invariably recognize the outrageousness of your behavior when things have reached a breaking point. I don't think I can count the number of times Tommy has appeared at my door with a plant, a spring flower arrangement, a note, a glass paperweight picked up at the local gift shop.

Usually, the only note with the gift is "Devotedly, Ben."
Sometimes it is an invitation to join you at one of those
black tie benefits you are forever giving money to, with a
scribble from you saying "Tommy will pick you up at six.
I'll assume it's OK unless I hear otherwise. Best, B."

When next we meet, a new issue has surfaced, and it
always has to do with a deep personal injury you feel one of
your children or one of your very special friends or partners
on Wall Street has inflicted.

Dear Ben, I wish I could help you with these severe
reactions. You are like a punching bag suspended by a long
cable. The slightest push sends you whirling through the
emotional air. You are always looking for affirmation from
those who are close to you. Disagreement on minor matters
feels like outright rejection to you, contrary to what you
say. You expect immediate and heartfelt gratitude for the
times when you give enormous help to one of your children
or one of your colleagues. When it isn't forthcoming as
swiftly and as warmly as possible, you are hurt, and when
expressions of gratitude arrive, you often feel they are not
commensurate with the size of your gift. Yet you are not
without insight into this pattern. You say to me from time
to time, "I know I'm cursed with an oversensitive nature."

That is true. All of us who love you would agree. I have
thought a long time about the roots of that oversensitivity.
There were three of you, growing up. I know both of your
brothers. Neither of them is afflicted with the extremities of
demand that characterize your personal relations. Each is
more task oriented than you are. Each is devoted to his
family and to you, but in each case their careers, their
clients, their patients, are at least as important to them in

their daily lives as their personal friendships are. For you, nothing can hold a candle to the flame of your devotion to the people who are close to you.

I do not wish to imply that your career has suffered because of your emotional needs. Not long ago, I had lunch with some of your treasured cronies at one of London's largest banking houses. All around the table, from a member of the House of Lords to the youngest, there was unanimous agreement about your genius in making judgments and predictions about trends in the market. I have also talked with people who have had their family fortunes in your care for as long as forty years, and counted themselves uncommonly lucky to have entrusted themselves to your direction. Your Phi Beta Kappa pin from Yale was fairly won. Your gifts of mental acuity, combined with an ability to read and retain information with amazing speed, made you a sure winner in your career from the beginning, and I think it says something important about you that instead of staying in the family firm, which has been operating on Wall Street for well over a century, you chose to make your way to the top in a firm altogether separate from family connections.

No, your oversensitivities couldn't have been due to a feeling that you had failed in your career. To my mind, you were phenomenally successful, both in terms of the loyalties of the people around you, from the back office boys to the senior partners, as well as in terms of financial gain. Yet, I guess we're none of us wholly satisfied with what we get.

I recall a luncheon at the Downtown Club. We were asking for a major gift from a mutual friend for a cause in which we were both involved. At the end of the lunch he

said, "Well, I'll give you $100,000 as a challenge gift."
You absolutely chortled with gleeful appreciation. Then
you said, "I'd give anything if I could make a gift like that
as casually as that!" I thought to myself that you got more
pleasure from giving $10,000 to someone you believe in
than our friend did from his offer of a challenge gift, but
you sincerely envied him.

Where did all that envy and sensitivity come from? It's
easy to say that there is an insatiable monstrous need in you
to be loved. When did that emotional hunger become so
hugely all-consuming? Your brothers don't labor under
such a burden. They have strong ties to family and friends,
but at the same time they are not excessively dependent
upon the approval and appreciation of people around them.
How did that prodigious dependence become so fixed in
you?

Your childhood was not strikingly different from that of
your brothers. I've seen pictures of you as a child. Your
mother wanted a daughter. She got a son, and so she kept
you in girlish garb beyond the usual years. Yet within the
context of your home, among all those servants and
caretakers, it was easy for a mother to dote on the child who
was only brought to her for inspection, approval, and
directions to the nanny who was in charge at the time.

Emotional deprivation is something we all experience.
Sometimes it is because the love that is given smothers us
and we fight to get our breath. For others, love is given in
such small measure that we starve for lack of it. For others,
love is a roller coaster. Now it is ecstatically abundant. We
feel recognized. Our wants are respected. Our needs are

provided for. The closeness we feel is pure heaven. Then, in a trice, it is gone. We are cast into a wasteland. It seems as though the rain will never come to make the desert bloom again.

Yet again, the love that is given us is more a fulfillment of our parents' needs than it is nourishment for us. We are seen as being needed instead of needing. The mother intensely wants the child's adoration and dependence. She thrives on it. Her unfulfilled emotional life is completed in the child. The consequence is a radiance that bedazzles the child and fills such children with unspeakable joy in giving their mother or father happiness. Such children will do anything to sustain it, and when it is withdrawn they are overwhelmed with fear and despair.

Dear Ben, the variations on this theme of emotional deprivation and its consequences are endless and infinitely complex. Every time you look at it carefully, it is like a kaleidoscope. There are constantly new patterns to be seen, new shapes and colors to be observed.

I don't know how to apply this insight to the journey of your soul, Ben. I remember when Mabel died you and I sat at midnight in your study, waiting for the undertaker to arrive. You gave me that look I have often seen on your face. I've seen it when you were in the hospital. I've seen it when you have handed me a letter from one of your grown children who had wounded you. I've seen it when for a number of reasons I failed to be there when you needed me. The look says "You've betrayed me. Life is grossly unfair. How could this happen to me? I don't deserve it. After all I've done for others, what good does it do?" It's the look of a little boy who feels he is being cruelly punished for something he didn't do. He expected to be loved. Instead, he was rejected.

I'm not going to psychologize your patterns of emotional reactions into the ground. Psychological patter bores me, but its truth cannot be avoided. Somewhere very early in your life you came to the fixed opinion that you were unlovable. Wanting voraciously to be loved, you failed to get the absolute affirmation of yourself you so hungrily sought from everyone. I don't know how or why that emotional dynamic started to animate your inner life, and I don't think you know. Nor am I willing to reduce it to some fatuous psychologism. All I can say is that it enslaves you to its wretched wheel again and again, and I wish I could help you to get free of its bludgeoning effects.

Your way of defending yourself against disappointment is to unload a pile of guilt on the people who fail to satisfy the appalling affirmation you require of us who love you. Do you realize how often you do that? I'm not the only person who has walked away from a tongue lashing from you with my tail between my legs, convinced that I had done some awful thing to you: I forgot to make a phone call you asked me to make. I neglected to write a letter you wanted me to write. I didn't get off a thank-you letter promptly enough for that neat nest of tables you sent to the house. I didn't sufficiently appreciate the profit you made for me when, on your advice, I bought some shares of a new stock the day it hit the market, and sold it two days later at a considerable gain, as you had predicted.

Those remembrances are peccadilloes compared to some accusations you often make toward Tommy and Della or to your children or to your partners. Everyone who loves you, Ben, has to carry your dark side at some time or other. It's your way of testing our devotion to you. You create a situation in which you virtually challenge us to reject you. Underneath it is hurt love crying out to be loved, while believing yourself to be unlovable. The result is a stalemate. We who love you are caught in the coils of our guilty resentments and you are caught in the coils of your frustrated anger. We then back off from each other for a cooling period, and in a short while the matter is forgotten. Life proceeds on its normal course again. Laughter and good conversation and relaxed occasions together resume their roles in our lives. If any of us try to raise the most recent issue of the past, we are told forcefully and finally, "Forget it, forget it. All is forgiven. It's water under the bridge." We put it behind us and life goes on quite happily until the next crisis comes, as it always does.

Now, if I haven't already lost you, I can hear you saying, "For God's sake, why are you spinning this tiresome web out so long? What's the point?" The point, dear Ben, is simply what does this pattern of relationship mean? What is it doing to your soul?

I'm glad I'm not beside you if you have gotten far enough to have read the last sentence. Your explosion must easily be heard throughout the neighborhood. "My soul! For Christ's sake, what has my soul got to do with it?"

Beloved friend, bear with me, I beseech you. Put the letter down now, if you must, but I beg you to hear me out when you have stopped being angry with me.

I can hear you sputtering, "But no one has ever spoken to me that way." Perhaps not, though I remember times when both your sons and your daughters have been even more direct with you than I have been. One letter, which you carried in your pocket for weeks, accused you of using your money to manipulate your children and to obtain your wishes. "They tell me love can't be bought!" "Do you think I try to buy their love?" you asked. "Well, you certainly have them intertwined in your head somehow," I answered. To which you responded in that low, hurt voice you sometimes use, "I thought you were my friend. Stop trying to take their side."

I am your friend, dear Ben, and that is the reason I am pleading with you to do something about your soul. None of us ever stands still in the spiritual realm. If we do, we will rot and decay in the place where we have planted our feet. We can go back, regression the books call it, or we can go forward. It's the going forward part that is the hardest, and that's what I implore you to try to do, painful though it is. Major changes in reshaping the soul are never easy.

I can hear your reaction to that one, too. "What? What? At seventy you think I can make major changes? Don't be ridiculous!" To which, dear friend, I say, "Yes, you can." I know some of the most crucial developments in my soul's journey came after I was sixty-five. To be sure, those changes would not have come had not my inner pain induced me to want them intensely, nor would my spiritual quest have taken on a new vitality had I not sought it with singleness of aim. Genuine inner change, the yeasty kind, which really raises the bread, never happens until we are ready to look inside and make a serious attempt to be truthful with ourselves, at fifty or at seventy.

I plead with you, Ben, to make the effort to deal with

your own inward truth. The salvation of your soul depends upon it. I refuse to believe that we are automatons determined to go on functioning the rest of our lives according to the way in which our inward machinery was bent and twisted in the first year or in the fifth, fifteenth, or thirtieth years of our lives. And the reason I don't believe it is that I have seen too many people change when some event, usually involving personal anguish, makes them pause in life's usual routine.

I call it a sacred pause. It is a still moment between the fading ticking of the past and the inexorable ticking of the future. I remember what a woman once said to me. She described a moment when she pulled into the driveway of her home immediately after her husband's arrival. She had just left an assignation with her lover. "My God, what am I doing with my life?" She sat in the car for an hour before going in. That was a sacred pause for her. In that still moment she knew she had to do something to change her life, and she did. Her family never knew it, but it was in that instant of inward truth that her family life was saved.

But I'm getting off the point, Ben. What I'm trying to say so circuitously is that at seventy you can begin to make changes in the essential character of your being that will make a difference for the rest of your life and beyond. Your life is full of crises, mostly generated by your own steam. When the next one comes along, perhaps one that puts you into the hospital wheezing and coughing to get your breath, consider the possibility (after the crisis is under control) that you are face-to-face with a sacred pause. A priceless opportunity has been placed in your hand to be used for change. Say to yourself, "I can go on like this from one crisis to the next, always projecting responsibility for my misery onto someone else, or I can make a commitment to truth, trying as sincerely as possible to accept my full share of responsibility for the mess I'm in. All I want to do is to deal with the truth about myself.''

Once you've made that commitment, perhaps in the days of recuperation in the hospital, write down for your eyes only, as clearly and honestly as possible, all the details of your most recent disappointment or your most recent feeling of betrayal. Above all, write about your feelings and your motives in the experience, all of them. Don't let any of them hide away in the corners of your remembrances. Look at them carefully. Reread what you have written. Hold those reflections as fully and clearly as possible before the divine consciousness. You will never believe it until you experience it, but there is a mysterious and breathtaking bond of fearful intimacy between each individual and the divine consciousness at such times. It hovers eternally behind the veil of your experience, waiting for the creature to recognize the figure of the creator whose other name is mercy. Once you have done that reverently, humbly, trustingly, quietly, a connection is made and a slow, sure transformation begins.

The great enemy of the transformation is guilt. What's done is done. It can't be undone, but guilt has the power to make bad things much worse. It can take a bad thing and inflate it beyond reality. I am not suggesting, Ben, that our misuse of one another, our presumptions and prevarications, our cruelties and gossipy tongues, are to be dismissed with the wave of a wand of forgetfulness. Transformation without integrity is impossible, and change without responsibility for our share in the tangled web of human relationships is a sham and a delusion.

Sorrow, real inward anguished sorrow for our part in the misery of others, is the indispensable prelude to the growth we seek. I wish I could generalize about how long that process of inward sorrow takes in the progress of the soul. It varies infinitely from person to person; weeks for some, months for others, even years now and then. All I know is that one day you wake up and you know it is time to move on. The agony is finished. The labor of the soul has prepared the ground for a new level of maturity. An impulse from the Christ breaks through the sorrow, and we have no question that the past now belongs to the past. Guilt has had its proper time and enough's enough.

I went through a period of sorrowful penitential remembrance not long ago. I told you about it. One sign that announced my forthcoming deliverance was a dream. I was in a grove of shady trees. It was a place that marks the ground where President James Buchanan was born. As a child I remember happy picnics in that sequestered park. My favorite food at those picnics was a chicken drumstick or, at the right season, a large, fully ripe peach. In my dream I was my present age, and I was leaning against a tree, eating the meat of a drumstick. Beside me was a large basket of fresh peaches. My beloved Aunt Mary was filling the air with her bright trilling laughter. She pointed to the peaches and said, "Those are all for you to take home." When I woke up, I knew the time for the singing of birds had come. The season of penitence was over. I was safely welcomed home again. I can't tell you, Ben, how earnestly I covet a process of growth along these lines for you. Really, dear man, you don't have to carry all that heavy baggage of guilt and defensiveness. It is time to claim freedom from your anxiety about not being liked and respected. The real you could step out into the sunshine of self-acceptance one day and realize that you are loaded with gifts of caring, generosity, kindness, humor, and wisdom, which you have never appreciated in yourself, although we who love you have told you these things repeatedly. I long to see you rest in those gifts of the spirit God gave you at the beginning. I yearn for the day to come when you are no longer bound to the seesaw of intense frustration and anger.

I pray for it fervently because I have seen you on countless occasions when the person God made you to be emerges, and I know that if that cherished person were to be in charge of your other self you would be engaged in the process of building more stately mansions of the soul here and now. It is not an insignificant undertaking!

May we talk about it soon?

With my love,

$$J^{+}$$

Dear Bill,

You have asked me, "As a recovered alcoholic, where do I go from here?" Let me think back a while on the journey we have shared.

One day, when you were a little child, I drove by your house. It was a warm spring day. The ground had just begun to breathe after winter's long grip. You had a toy set of garden tools spread out before you. You picked up the hoe and began to attack the lawn in front of your porch with all the power your young body possessed. I stopped to watch you. Your face was filled with intense rage and determination. You beat the ground relentlessly.

As I drove down the street, I wondered what it was that my young friend Billy was so angry about. In all the years we have known each other, I've never forgotten the fierce anger I saw on your face that day when you were but a child at the end of your first year of school.

Bill, you were an original. From the beginning it was extraordinary. You were a natural magnet around whom your friends revolved. You set the pace. The other kids imitated you in everything, even in the styles of clothes you wore. They competed to be on your team. Your talents were abundant. Coordination was as simple to you as walking. It was a wonder to watch you on skates, under all that padding and helmet, weaving your way down the hockey rink with your stick in perfect control of the puck, and you were only twelve years old!

Your grace on the playing field was always there, no matter whether the sport was hockey, soccer, or lacrosse. I used to go to the games when you became a high schooler just to watch you. The only thing that ever seemed to shake your amazing skill was fatigue. I could see it creep up on you. I would become impatient with the coach for not taking you out of the game, even though I realized he was depending on you to win the match for him.

Whatever happened to change all that when you went away to college? I remember you as a sophomore in college. I was in Boston on a mission for one of the churches. I called you to arrange a luncheon. As you walked toward my table in the restaurant, I barely recognized you. Your face was ravaged. I wondered how much weight you must have lost. Your blond hair was stringy and dank. You reeked of alcohol. We both hid behind heartiness. We played the game of pretending everything was as it always had been. You drank gin as though you had just come in from a stinking desert. We were both glad when the lunch was over.

You left the table first. I tarried over another cup of coffee. "What has happened to him?" I kept asking myself. I wasn't proud of myself. I had pulled one of my head-in-the-sand routines. The red-hot questions in my mind had gone unasked. I chickened out. It just wasn't in me to raise the issue that was uppermost in my heart. All I kept saying to myself was "What drug is he on? Where is that happy, well-liked, highly successful kid I knew all those years?"

In all candor, Bill, even today, years later, after all the talking we've done, I still fail to understand the metamorphosis from your high school years to your college years.

You've given me many clues, but the change in you is still a mystery to me! I can see you raising your eyebrows. You and I have established many connections between your patterns of behavior, your addictions, and your life story, but human personality can never be reduced to a series of causes and effects, no matter how clear and incontrovertible they happen to be. However, I don't wish to minimize the insights we have been given. They were painful and they were blessed. You are the whole person you are today partly because you walked back over the private mine field of your early life.

Your father's alcoholism and your mother's adulation would make a vulnerable mixture for any son to endure. I am convinced you survived successfully as a growing kid because you were exceptionally gifted, mentally and physically, and because you developed the knack to a high degree of efficiency, of repressing negative energy.

I hate to think of your defenseless years in that lovely house of yours. With most alcoholics there is a breakpoint. It is the moment when rational behavior succumbs to the power of irrationality. Your father experienced many breakpoints as an alcoholic. He was intensely jealous of you from the beginning of your life. As you grew older he couldn't resist the need to pick a quarrel with you, which always ended in a frenzied moment when he unbuckled his belt and let you have it.

Your mother's reaction was to wait it out until the house was quiet. Your father slept in a fetuslike position on the sofa of his den. Then she would creep into your bed. We have spoken of the fetish you have about silken lingerie. How could it be otherwise? You were bound to associate warmth and comfort and sensuality with a feminine presence lightly clad in silk.

It seems incredible, but that pattern in your house persisted, if I remember rightly, through your high school years. Your father's alcoholic outbursts and irrationality became fixed on many people. As time went on, your mother took more and more of his abuse, but didn't you tell me that you have several memories of a repetition of her old pattern, even in your junior and senior years of high school?

The capacity most of us have to compartmentalize our emotions is appalling. Yet without it, how would we survive? If I had to carry all the traumas and failures of my past in the forefront of my consciousness every day of my life, I would have been dead long ago. Forgetfulness can be a gift of grace.

And so, I wonder how you would have lived through your early life without an ability to put negative reality out of your mind. Fortunately, you were bright and good-looking. You were popular as a friend and as a star on the playing field. You had material advantages not many of your peers could match. How well I remember your first convertible!

The compensations were many. Yet you and I know the

wounds of your father's abuse and your mother's intimacy contributed to an infection of the soul from which you are still recovering at the age of thirty-five.

If I didn't know my own early life so well, I would find it difficult to understand how you were able to keep all that traumatic experience to yourself. It was a secret nightlife you never talked about to anyone until we began to share many things five years ago. I'll always treasure the confidence that has opened us to one another, Bill. Nothing I can say could thank you enough for the gift of trust between us.

What was the bond that kept us in touch all those years before we were really open and honest with each other? It is easy to say that I filled a vacuum in your soul. It is equally obvious that you never lost a certain innate kindness and dignity, which never failed to draw me to you. I also sensed the depth of your need for me and your devotion to me. Bill, you must know by now that it was not a one-way street from your heart to mine. Your unfailing compassion and charm have brought a host of friends to you. I am simply thankful to be one of them. My only regret is that the way didn't open for us to share real feeling and past traumas until you entered AA. Yet there was no doubt about our devotion to one another. Separation by time or distance never altered it.

It was threatened though, wasn't it, when I used every resource at my command to pressure you into the hospital? I really thought you were going to attack me just before we went into the admissions building.

You were in high gear that day. I was frightened. You could easily have killed both of us as we tore down Storrow

Drive in your car. Of course, at that moment you thought we were simply going for a consultation with a physician with wide experience in the treatment of alcohol and drug addiction. Nevertheless, you resented me with every cell of your body because I had wheedled you into an agreement to talk with him.

I was never sure at what moment you realized what you were faced with. I think it was after we left the doctor's office and you glanced up at the sign above the hospital door. It said Admissions Building. I knew then that if you chose to run for the car, I would be helpless to prevent your escape. You were clearly furious with me, but you were also listening to my pleas. Was it our friendship that kept you moving with me up those steps, or was it a small voice that said, "Joe is right. I know I'm sick. I'm going to destroy myself if I go on the way I'm living now." I suppose it was both, but I wonder how you kept moving into the building when the clashing cymbals in your head were shouting "Run, run!"

It still seems like a miracle to me that you signed yourself in, and that you stayed in the hospital for the full three weeks agreed upon. I had prayed for it vehemently, but I also knew something of the mammoth power of your resistance. Three weeks is not a long stretch of time to reach someone who is addicted to alcohol or any other drug, but it was long enough to detoxify your system and to introduce you to AA. Ten years of extreme dependence on alcohol are not broken in three weeks of treatment by someone who resists the program, as you did in the secret parts of your mind, every step of the way.

I knew it before the period was over. On both of my

visits to you at the hospital, I realized intuitively that you were only marking time until you could fulfill your agreement and head for the nearest liquor store. I rejected that intuition at the time because I desperately wanted the program to succeed. When it didn't, though, I wasn't surprised. The one solid gain from that experience, however, was your exposure to a light at the end of the tunnel, wasn't it? After that hospitalization you knew there was help when you were ready to choose it, and you knew the people in the treatment center were humane, compassionate, and tough.

It was almost two years later that you went back to them. I'm really not clear what it was that compelled you to commit yourself to their care. Was it the accident that winter? Or was it the paltry life-style you couldn't endure any longer—empty, weary, guilt-ridden, being afraid, hiding behind false masks of pretended cordiality and competence, unable to bear the company of anyone from your early life, comfortable only with people who were at the opposite end of the social spectrum from the one in which you were brought up? I suppose it was all of that, and much more than you've ever told me. All I know is the summer when you really reached for wholeness and subsequently became a serious and faithful member of AA is the summer when my heart began to sing. The lost was found. You walked out of the valley of the shadow of death into the world of life and light again.

I shall never forget all the surprises of joy you experienced that first year. You kept telling me on the telephone, "It's like I never saw autumn foliage before in my life. The colors are incredible. I want to shout to everyone on the street, 'Look, look, don't you see how beautiful that is?'''

It was like that all through the year. Do you remember telling me how you rolled down a hill near your apartment building after a snowstorm, blinded by the whiteness, laughing and kicking your feet all the way down? People became important to you again, not because you needed them as actors on your private stage of misery to fulfill your alcoholic fantasies or your sexual demands, but because you were as interested in giving respect as you were eager to receive it. The transformation of your consciousness left no aspect of your life untouched. The flame of a cardinal winging its way through the blue sky, or an apple tree in blossom, was like a miracle that had never happened since the first day of creation. What an unmitigated joy it was to be around you during your first year of freedom!

It still is, dear Bill, and always will be, but I'm sure you'll agree that initial burst from the prison house of violence and guilt was something quite special.

In the last couple of years we've had a lot of good stuff and bad stuff to sort out. I admire the way you have insisted on understanding what your decade of acute alcoholism was all about. AA has been our rock. Without their support and their program, we would never have made it, but after you committed yourself to sobriety, you went another step and committed yourself to forgiveness. We both know that cheap forgiveness is a fake. The real thing is always costly.

I remember the pain you felt as you dealt directly with your father. Neither of us expected your father's reaction. He made a great show of his approval and pleasure in your decision to admit yourself to the hospital for treatment. He highly praised your regularity at AA meetings. I thought I had prepared him for your candor about the past. He encouraged me to believe he would welcome an open discussion about your relationship.

As I think about it now, I realize he must have thought you were going to apologize for your treatment of him in the past ten or twelve years. He made a passing reference to all the money he had spent on you during those years, but it was said as if a joke. I should have known better. I'm afraid my sanguine temperament tripped me up. The kind of discussion you planned to have with him was loaded with fireworks. I failed to see that.

In any case, you persevered. I wish I could have seen his face when you said, "You punished me with your belt when I was a kid, and I punished you with the bottle when I was a man; and now it's time we both stopped punishing each other. You made me feel I was a rotten, no-good kid, and I believed you. After all, you were my father! I had to prove to the world that you were right. In the last ten years I gave you plenty of reason to be ashamed of me, but, believe me, that was nothing compared to the shame I felt about myself. I almost suffocated under a garbage load of guilt as big as a mountain. It's time we started to forgive each other."

That was quite a speech, Bill, if I have recorded it rightly. A strangely powerful link gets forged between the tormented and the tormentor. Your father wasn't ready to break the link. You were. He still needs you as a tormentor to satisfy his unrecognized guilt. He secretly envies your freedom from alcohol. He has never been able to do what you have done because he doesn't think he is addicted. It was intolerable to him to think his treatment of you as a growing child had anything to do with your behavior in the past ten years. He is not only still in bondage to alcohol but is still enslaved by his need to torment and to be tormented. Not a few of us find it easier to make others miserable and to make ourselves miserable than to do something constructive about our misery.

I can hear his voice, "Why, you goddamned sniveling ungrateful kid! After all I've done for you, bailing you out of jail, wiring you money in California, sending you to a damn fine college, which sure as hell was money down the drain! You cheated and drank yourself through four years of a wasted life. How do you figure I'm supposed to get down on my knees and beg your forgiveness?"

When you quietly walked out of the door an hour later, Bill, you turned your back on the enslaving power of a love which wallows in tormenting and being tormented. Guilt feeds upon guilt, and the result is a monstrous distortion of love. You have forgiven him the painful way. It wasn't enough to understand him or to understand yourself, as an alcoholic and as a person. You went all the way. You even told him you understood his rage, because you had lived with anger in yourself as long as you could remember.

I don't recall everything you shared with me of that encounter, but I do know that there was an unforgettable look of peace and self-assurance on your face when next we met. It was a breakthrough of the soul.

I don't know how much longer your father will insist on his pattern of denial. We both wish it could be broken, but it is not within our power or the province of our responsibility to do it. You know better than I that he is the only one who can do it. He may go the rest of his life frozen in his justifications and self-deceptions. Who knows where the need to deny comes from? If we could lift the curtain of his consciousness, long since forgotten, I suspect we would come away weeping with sorrow and love for him. The only positive element we both agree upon is that his money has protected him from having to sink to the levels of self-hatred and degradation that left horrendous scars on your soul.

I wish I knew what to say about your relation to your mother. I agree that however twisted her mothering of you was, her love of you knew no bounds. In all these years she has always been there for you.

There were times, I'm sure, in your alcoholism when you wanted her to define limits and to resist your manipulations. You knew you could get anything out of her you wanted. You also knew you would feel guilty every time you lied to her, or turned your charm on her to obtain your ends. Your pockets were seldom empty of her generosity.

You frequently tell me how unspeakably light you feel since you no longer carry a leaden weight of guilt on your back for the conflict and resentment you felt toward your father, but, Bill, I suspect the conflict you feel toward your mother is laden with even greater complexity and guilt. The women in your life have paid a terrible price for that complexity. All of us do harm to others according to the harm done to us. The ambivalence you felt toward your mother has been transferred to the people you love. You swing between opposites of devotion and distance, oftentimes without warning and in the course of a few hours. The depth of that conflict has prevented you from making a commitment to anyone. You get close to it, but when real intimacy and openness are required, you back off.

I am puzzled by the people you have lived with. They are invariably from the bottom of the ladder. The differences in education, appearance, age, sophistication, privilege, are striking. They are good people in their own way, but I have wondered many times what you had in common with them other than sex and drink. Their dependence on you is extreme, and in a curious way your need of each of them as they have succeeded one another in your life is also extreme. There is something pathetic about it. Each of you makes excessive demands on the other for time and sex, but neither of you meet one another as persons, growing together and sharing common interests. I get the impression that you never talk about feelings; at least not until a new person comes into your life and emotions are released by the white-hot fuse of jealousy and recrimination.

Sobriety, as is so frequently the case, has done little to change these patterns. You will object to that observation! And you are right to do so, Bill, because there is the big difference that you now live alone. Your partners come and go, but they don't live with you any more. In addition, you have now held the same job for three years, and your apartment looks like you again. The books and records, the tapes and furniture, reflect the taste of a person of great richness of mind and spirit. Those are big differences. They have come only with the sobriety you have labored intensely to maintain, with the help of AA.

Yet when it comes to the quality of your personal relationships, it is the same. You seek out losers who cling to you and you to them. It's safer that way. Nothing in your emotional geography is threatened. It's more comfortable that way, isn't it?

Bill, you could live the rest of your life in this style. The income you have from the family, plus your income from your job, could support you in the way you want to live, indefinitely. However, you have asked, "Where do I go from here?" I sense you want to move on to a new, more stable, and satisfying existence. If that is true, two things seem essential to me.

One has to do with your relation to your mother. It is infinitely complex. When I ponder it, I realize quickly that I am out of my depth. The consequences of your relationship are obvious, and I know you want to cut the cord of your dependence on her; but every time we have approached that problem in our talks I see great pain in your face. Good-bye is the hardest word in the human language, as you have often heard me say. Yet this is one relation that can only be changed when you find the courage to relinquish it. Until you do, your soul will remain unmended, torn, and conflicted.

As with sobriety, I don't think this is a goal you can achieve alone. Give yourself the gift of some solid therapy. I have some names I can recommend to you. When we talked about this route previously, you turned me down. I have not pressed it, but I have a strong feeling now is the time. I yearn to see you claim another giant step of freedom from the bondage of the past.

The other thing has to do with your spiritual quest. As

you know, I have had a confessor whose guidance has been indispensable to my journey of the soul. I am also committed to the regular practice of morning prayer and meditation. The waters of my soul would have long since become stagnant without those disciplines, bit I can't make it alone. I need a friend, a prayer partner, the fellowship of a faithful, like-minded prayer group, or a spiritual director, if my journey is to avoid dead-end byways. Sometimes I have availed myself of all these resources, but mostly I have settled on a mutually trusting and caring prayer partnership.

My recommendation to you, Bill, is that you seek a spiritual director. I beg you to consider this possibility, regardless of your decision about therapy. There is an abundance of healing energy waiting for you through such a discipline.

Naturally, I would love to be your spiritual director. What a joy it would be for me to share in the healing labor of the wounds of your past. I haven't any doubt it would happen in time.

However, I'm afraid we're too close to one another. I am associated with almost all the memories you have of your early life. The effectiveness of a spiritual director is not promising if the relation is one of previous attachment. Some distance is needed if the perspective of both parties is to be true. Without the grace of humble detachment, there is a certain astringency that is fatally absent.

When spiritual directors take on a soul for mending and molding, we need a firm hand and an unclouded vision free of former negatives and positive emotions.

There is a priest within easy driving distance of your office whose gifts and training I greatly admire as a spiritual director. When she found it almost impossible to obtain a parish, she embarked on a training program for this ministry. It has proved to be a use of her talents that exceeds anything she ever dreamed to be possible. She is a natural as a spiritual director. Her warmth, her depth of spiritual knowledge, her sensitivity and maturity, offer you much promise for the mending of your soul.

One of the great positives in your life story, Bill, is the way you have always loved the church and the way in which you have been blessed by the church. Thank God, I am not the only pastor who has shepherded your soul. Your cup overflows. I don't know how you were blessed by so many wonderful people among ministers. Doubtless it has something to do with the charm and humility everyone sees in you, but whatever it is, I'm grateful, because it is through the church that you have never lost touch with the ultimate search for life's meaning. Even in the worst days of your alcoholism you knew the church was your haven and your hope.

Well, I guess that's all I have to say for now. I won't apologize for the length of this letter, because you asked for it! I know you will think long and hard about both of my suggestions. Let me hear from you soon.

With my love and prayers,

Dear Jennifer,

Love plays tricks with our minds. Rationality and irrationality become hopelessly mixed up with one another. I have stood in a valley between the heights of two Swiss Alps and listened to several singers bouncing their voices from opposite mountain walls. The clash and confusion of the sounds make you dizzy.

Sometimes two people in love with one another, especially when it is outside their marriage, hear so many voices calling for their attention that they are soon lost in a cacophony of hopeless contradictions. My heart fairly stops in the midst of these cross currents. Can we find a foothold by standing on solid fact?

Jennifer, after listening many hours to your struggles with Ted, the hard truth I beg you to accept is that he doesn't want to leave his marriage and he doesn't want you to leave your marriage. He likes it just the way it is. Can you assimilate that fact? Are you willing to accept the implications of that position? I hope I'm not being too harsh. The last thing I want to do is to contribute one more ounce to your pain. Yet, sometimes the wound has to be lanced before it can heal. You have resisted facing this fact for five years. The time has come to deal with it.

I quake when I think of the danger this love has brought to your soul. This is a concern that has crushed me almost to the point of suffocation ever since we first began to talk. I have withheld any discussion about the dangers because I knew you were not ready to face them. I have waited and prayed year after year. Now we are soon into the sixth year. Recently you have given me more and more signs that tell me you are at an important juncture in the twists and turns of this painful ecstasy.

I have refrained from raising spiritual issues in connection with this relationship because I was afraid I would lose you. People have to do what they have to do until they are ready to change. (That's a frightful jumble of words, isn't it? But I know the meaning.) All of us do things that are stupid and contrary to our own best interests. We pursue a path clearly contrary to our happiness. We undertake a relationship that threatens our future and that is blatantly opposed to the moral standard we espouse.

I have seen it happen dozens of times. No amount of well-intentioned advice makes the slighest difference. No pressure of a negative or moral character changes the course of events. It seems there is little any of us can do except to wait it out until there is a catastrophe or until someone reaches a point of painful exhaustion and disillusionment. In the meantime, the best thing real friends can do is to stand by loyally and closely with love and patience. The last remedy is to chatter about it, or to make judgments and register moralistic disapproval. That only succeeds in making the situation worse and in removing ourselves as friends from the scene.

So, Jennifer, I have waited and prayed and prayed and waited, yearning for an opening that would give us a chance to deal creatively with the complexity of this experience before calamity struck and before you were ravaged by bitter disappointment. On your last visit you said with resigned bone weariness, "I don't think I can go on with this any longer."

As you left my study, I knew the opening I had prayed for was at hand, and now that you are on vacation I have a perfect opportunity to put concerns on paper. Letters have the advantage of allowing us to review what has been said and to reflect on the truth or nontruth of it.

Let's begin at the beginning. It all began at the hospital, didn't it? I mean, you would not have met Ted if you hadn't been a nurse and he a practicing surgeon on the staff. There is a special comaraderie in an operating room. He admired your skills as an OR nurse and you admired his sure and deft techniques as a surgeon. He saw the way you handled pressure with poise and unflagging devotion to the patient. You watched the compassion he brought to anxious families. You quickly worked together as a beautiful team, each knowing what the other would do almost before it was done. It was as natural as the rising of the sun that you should have formed a relation deeper than ordinary friendship. It happens in the working world all the time. I'm sure Ted is not the only physician with whom you have formed a bond of mutual admiration. What made Ted different?

I believe it was the accident of an unconscious fit.

Something in Ted instinctively recognized something in you which was perfectly tailored to an unconscious need in him; you recognized something in Ted that represented an unfulfilled need in your unconscious. People call it chemistry, but the thing is more complex than that.

There are dozens of factors, but the deepest is at the level of the unconscious. A particular woman comes into a man's life at middle age. She embodies an image of beauty and style that perfectly fits a long-forgotten myth of his early experience. He has little awareness of this connection, but her voice, her manner, her coloring, her figure, her taste, her background, her values, fulfill his myth with shattering power. If his marriage has lost its vitality, if it is no longer fulfilling, if it has become a disparate relationship in which one party has moved far ahead of the other party in knowledge, sophistication, or interests, then in today's world of freedom and opportunity he is a grossly vulnerable man. Should some woman become a part of his life through natural association and friendship under these circumstances, and should she happen to fulfill the mythic figure of a lover in his unconscious, you can be sure that something enormously powerful is going to be triggered in that man's psyche.

Jennifer, I could easily reverse the scenario. The identical process happens to women, as you know in depth. You are extraordinarily vulnerable. Your husband is a good man, but I have often wondered why you married him. Was it that he happened to be the likeliest candidate at the time when everyone expected you to marry? You are still a beautiful woman. I can easily imagine how eager he was to lock you into marriage. People often stumble into marriage without knowing what they are doing. Society expects marriage, and people conform. Many friends of my generation married in order to get away from home, although they didn't know it at the time. Your childhood was filled with intense conflict and confusion. It was natural that you sought someone to deliver you from that environment as soon as you graduated from Cornell School of Nursing.

Now, Ted fulfills longings you couldn't possibly describe. He brings breadth and height and depth to your life. He has introduced you to new interests, new places, new people, new ways of looking at things, new horizons of expectation. He is exciting to be with, his money makes possible a host of options you never dreamt of, and his decisiveness and macho confidence are a constant challenge to your not inconsiderable energies.

There is a little boy in him only you have seen, and I suspect there have been some lyrically precious hours of utter quietness when you have held him on your breast in a time of unspeakable peace. He is the man you have always wanted, consciously and unconsciously, and you are the woman he has always wanted but didn't know it.

Now we come to the painful part. The circumstances are in sharp contrast. You have one child who will graduate from high school next year. Ted has six children. The youngest is in the fifth grade; the oldest will soon enter medical school. Your husband's dependence on you is extreme. I wonder if he would survive without you. Ted's wife is like granite. He knows she would stop at nothing to get everything he owns, and more, if he should sue for divorce. He likes money and all the power it commands. He

Jennifer

45

also enjoys the social position his wife's family provides him in New York society, and his children mean more to him than anything in the world. The difference in the circumstances of you two people is startling.

It troubles me that your hold on him is as sexual as it is. There can't be a nook or a cranny in that hospital where you haven't made love. The frequency and variety of your assignations defy belief.

The sexual character of an extramarital relation often reflects an intensity and an ecstasy of fulfillment not known previously by the partners. Yours is no exception. There are countless facets to loving and being loved in bed between two persons who commit themselves to each other outside of their respective marriages. The name for it is adultery, but as soon as the word is used, the complexity of the experience is dismissed. Morality cleaves the air with its righteousness. Discussion dries up. The parties involved withdraw from the discussion, but not from their bed.

Nevertheless, Jennifer, I do use the word. There is no other. The moral dimension has to be faced. As you will see in a moment, I do empathize with the complexity of the sexual relation with sincere compassion, but first let us deal with the question of responsibility. The essence of the problem is this: are we responsible for one another or are we not?

In the final accounting, each of us is ultimately responsible for himself or herself. The design of the fabric of intimacy we weave with the variegated colors of our loving is our own making. We choose the quality of the threads we use. We tie the knots. We determine the beauty or the ugliness of the result. We can give the cloth little care. We

can ignore its torn and tattered fringes, or we can mend it.
We can also weave a cloth of gold that lasts beyond a
lifetime. We do the weaving, not fate, nor coincidental
circumstances. We do the choosing. God refuses to do it for
us. No one can be accountable for us but ourselves.

However, as you well know, Jennifer, accountability
doesn't stop at our door as a lonely traveler. He always
comes with many questions. As he knocks on the leafy door
of our souls, the ultimate question may be "What did you
do with what I gave you?" No sooner is the question posed
than others step forward to claim their truth: "What was
your part in the suffering of this person, of that family, of
the horrible event no one will ever forget, of the evil that
brought the downfall of the institution where you
worked?" And so on. It is all one bundle. There is no
escape from the unity of responsibility. We are forever
bound up with the people and the events in which we have
played important roles in the denouement of destiny. It
cannot be escaped. Souls are not shaped in isolation.

The consciousness of the Creator exceeds by
unnumbered miles even the most sophisticated computer
imaginable. Between our consciousness and the divine
consciousness there is an intimacy and extensiveness of
knowledge, which is breathtaking to the modern mind
when it is taken seriously.

But who takes this consciousness seriously today? Do
we not do everything in our power to deny it because such a
possibility is too threatening to our comfortable self-serving
orientation to the world? We are sure divine omniscience is
a hangover of mediaeval superstition. Science has banished
it. We are no longer responsible to God for what we do or

for what we fail to do. The morality of God is a meaningless phrase. We don't believe in it. What is the consequence of that banishment?

Erase the experience of the sacred from human consciousness, Jennifer, and it follows, as the day follows the night, that you will erase a sense of the sacredness of every human being from our consciousness. When we have no fear of God, human relations become a jungle in which the only law that prevails is the survival of the fittest. There are no absolutes that judge us and preserve civilized society. Everything becomes relative to the situation in which the act occurs or in which the word is spoken. All things are justified. Means and ends become disastrously disconnected. Anything justifies anything, all the way from detention camps in Siberia to adultery in the suburbs of America. "The center cannot hold."

To be sure, I recognize that there are vast differences between the imprisonment of Sakharov and an extramarital relationship in Lake Forest, but the same kind of thinking leads to both results. In one case it is the protection of the state. In the other it is the happiness and fulfillment of the two parties involved. Yet in both, the responsible people feel they are justified in the pain they may bring to others. I'm afraid, though, the sad truth is that in both cases the odds are great that none of the responsible people have given the question of accountability any agonized reflection at all.

But you are different, Jennifer. From the beginning of this liaison with Ted, you have been obsessed with the moral issue. For the first three years you hid behind the justification that Ted's growth in this incarnation of his soul had to go through this madness and that you were the midwife to deliver him from his hedonism in preparation for his next journey on this earth!

When the moment came that you knew you were up to your eyeballs in your passionate commitment to Ted, the world almost fell apart. You had to face the realization that you were as responsible for the adultery as Ted was. Since then, I have stood by while you fought yourself. I was not surprised when your affair became an on-again, off-again thing. How many times have you tried to break it? I'm sure you have lost count. Last summer I saw you rapidly losing weight. Your face was a haunted mask. I thought you were headed for a serious illness.

Christmas was the turning point, wasn't it? You were on vacation and Ted took off a fortnight. It must have cost him a mint to have taken that crew, including his parents and his in-laws, to Eleuthera for Christmas. He didn't call, and he didn't come home three days early to spend them with you as you had both planned. I knew then we were going to have a showdown. I doubt if you had previously allowed yourself to face how shoddily you had been used or how much your self-respect had been degraded.

That New Year's Day when you wept and wept in my study you alarmed me. I wondered what would happen. When you left, you hugged me and said, "Don't worry, I'll make it." Intuitively, I knew you would. Later I realized my confidence was based on a vague but real sense that you were in touch with your moral depths again. Something stronger than emotion and rationality was taking over. I knew the end was in sight.

The next week when we talked I was not surprised

when you said, "Well, it's done. I've quit my job and I've cut the umbilical cord to Ted." Nor have I been surprised that in recent months you have seen him briefly. He is nothing if not importunate. I don't know what you can do short of changing your phone to an unlisted number and varying your routine, all of which you've done. "He doesn't love me. He only needs me," you tell me repeatedly. I think that's true, but I wonder if Ted knows how to love anyone. One exception may be his youngest, handicapped daughter. Remember when I made that casual call on Ted's home? I asked his wife, "When does Ted bleed?" Her answer was "Oh, let anything happen to Sherry and he'll bleed all over the living room rug."

Ambivalence is inevitable, Jennifer, in breaking a relationship as strong as this one is. Anticipate it in yourself and be patient, but don't lose your grip on the truth of the situation. Your myth is that Ted will suffer so much without you he will eventually sacrifice his home for you. As I say, Jennifer, I don't think Ted will ever do it, and lately I've wondered if your conscience would let you get away with it. I felt the intensity of your empathy for Sherry's all-emcompassing handicap. Isn't it interesting that Ted is unreservedly devoted to her? It gives me hope for him, but what would you do with your guilt as you faced Sherry's suffering due to her father's absence? You can be sure her mother would use Sherry as a conduit for her anger at both you and Ted. She would find a host of excuses for refusing Ted visiting privileges with Sherry. It would be only one way of punishing both you and Ted. Every day there would be another. He in turn would begin to retaliate by withholding support money. On and on it would go. Could you handle that, Jennifer? I doubt it.

Now we come to the present moment, Jennifer. When you said to me, "I don't think I can go on with this," I knew a powerful impulse was surfacing in you. It is a strong influence in your inward self. It is what took you into graduate nursing. It is what has made you the reliable and caring nurse you are. It must have been the source of your sanity these past five years. I have been awed by the way you have kept your family nourished and at peace while all that has been going on. The moral sense in you is powerful. It motivates you more than you realize. You are now at a golden moment in your journey, Jennifer.

If you can allow the morality of the situation to lead you back to the Father's house, a major breakthrough for the growth of your soul is at hand. A strong moral sense is a surefooted handmaiden of the Lord. We don't find the Father's house without her. It isn't always easy to choose the trail she blazes. Sometimes her signs are many and different. Truth leads one way. Love points another. We search painfully for a place where the two coincide. Finally we throw ourselves on the mercy of God and take the path that fulfills our responsibility to the greatest possible good, praying that God will bless it.

Earlier in this letter, Jennifer, you will remember I referred to the incredibly intimate and relentless bond of omniscience, which binds our little consciousness to the divine consciousness. Every religion in history and every authentic experience of God bear unanimous witness to the unnameable holiness of God. It is the essence of the Divine represented to Moses as a holy mountain, which the children of Israel touch only at the peril of their lives; in the Gospels by that blinding abyss of light the chosen three saw transfiguring the image of Christ on Mount Tabor; or by the beloved Mary in the Easter garden when she was told, "Don't touch me—".

Morality, an unflinching acceptance of responsibility for the persons we become, is the vestibule of the Father's house. It cannot be entered by any other door. Before we come to the holy mountain there is a process of grieving in the soul for opportunities missed and for hurts we inflicted. It cannot be avoided. It is a purifying fire, which truth requires in preparation for the holy place. I know not where or when. I only know it is a process no one escapes in the soul's journey.

It is here that the Christ Event becomes our lifeline. Morality without spirituality is an impotent, heavy burden that produces a fruitless righteousness. The world is, however, blessed by such moral folk. Their integrity and unswerving sense of duty have saved the pillars of civilization more than once, but the thing has little staying power. It withers and dies with that great generation that was steeped in its Calvinist strictures. Unless morality is lifted into the realm of the transcendent, it loses its living power. All that is left is a wearisome, necessary litigiousness.

In the Goetheanum, the temple of the devotees of Rudolph Steiner in Switzerland, there is a powerful Christ figure, carved of wood. It is mammoth in size. At the feet of the Redeemer there is a confused mass of tortured creatures from the human and animal world. One sacred hand reaches downward toward the struggling masses,

drawing them magnetlike up and through himself to his
other upward-reaching hand, which releases them into a
sphere of transcendent glory and freedom. Human
consciousness with all its plans and contradictions and
weighty self-centeredness and sinful rebelliousness is
transformed through this God-man. But it isn't done en
masse. We come into the world one by one. Each of us is
accountable for himself, including the scars and wounds we
have inflicted on the souls of others.

It would be a hopeless prospect, Jennifer, wouldn't it, if
the visible image of the invisible had not been disclosed to us
as an unconditional being of unimaginably boundless love
and mercy brooding over his creation since the beginning of
the universe? It is Golgatha and the Christ Event that rent
the veil of the temple, revealing its secrets for all time. No
wonder our Easter songs burst the seams of joy, and bells
peal their praise. ''What language shall I borrow to thank
thee, dearest friend?''

The present hour is pregnant with new life for you.
Thank God for the few glimpses of peace that have been
given. I covet many more of them. We have much to talk
about, how those states of peace and forgiveness can be
retrieved and integrated into your new life. You know, I'm
sure, that things will never be the same, and we need to
pray and talk about how that is to be managed.

Meanwhile, my dear, I want you to accept one discipline
while you are in Florida. St. John's Cathedral is not more
than a thirty mile drive from you. I beg you to take the
sacrament at early Eucharist every morning until your
return. Sometimes you will feel burdened by the routine of
the liturgy, and various good reasons will conspire to

discourage you from doing it. But persevere. Don't let anything interfere with this discipline. By the time you come home you will say to me, ''The Eucharist, the Eucharist, how did I live so long without it?''

Other than that, Jennifer, relax, get some sunshine, have some fun, and let the peace of God keep you in the mercy of his holy streams.

With my love,

Joe +

Dear Charlotte,

It was almost as much of a shock to me as it was to you. After all these years of sharing the sorrow and the rage of many divorces, I well know there is no such thing as a perfect marriage, but I certainly thought yours was close to one.

The thing which is unique to your experience of divorce, in so far as I know, is the suddenness of it. If I understand you rightly, you went to bed with Bud feeling serene and loving. He awakened you in the middle of the night with affection. He made wildly intense love to you, and the next morning after breakfast he told you that he had packed an overnight bag, he was leaving you, and he would be back for the rest of his clothing after the weekend.

It baffles me even as it has crushed you. I can't get my thought around it. If your marriage had a history of tension, withdrawal, hostility, deception, infidelity, or even elemental incompatibility of temperaments separated by a wide diversity of interests, I could make some sense out of this precipitate action; but when I've been in your home, the pleasure of being with both of you was greatly magnified by the obvious way in which your marriage was not only one of love and mutual devotion, but one in which you were transparently involved in one another's interests, mutually supportive. Bud was hugely proud of your accomplishments in real estate. He often said, "She's a natural at it," and you never failed to find an opportunity to affirm him in his profession as a pediatrician. You both began as neophytes in the history of painting, but within a few years you were equally knowledgeable and enthusiastic about the field. You like the same kind of people. You enjoy the same recreational outlets. You are both snobs, but the nice kind! By that I don't mean that you consider yourselves superior to other people, but simply that you have very sophisticated tastes not many people share. I see it in the kinds of books you both read and in the elegance that characterizes your style of life.

Of course, we have all thought it was such a pity that you have had no children. Bud would be as caring a father as I can imagine, and you would be super as a mother. However, Bud's great success in his profession is in part, don't you think, due to the way in which he pours his parenting instincts into his treatment of all those kids he sees in his office and in the hospital. Your nurturing instincts have been concentrated in taking care of Bud as devotedly and unreservedly as possible. Don't mistake my meaning. To my observation, you always seemed very much a woman, a lover, a companion to Bud, not a fluttering mother figure handing him a glass of beer or bedroom slippers when he needed them. Yet I think you'll agree your nurturing energies have always centered on Bud, and he has blossomed under them.

How can such a thing be? This sudden departure defies my comprehension. You tell me that all you are able to get out of him is that he says he just isn't "in love" with you any more. I wish I had a ten dollar bill for each time I have heard that declaration. How does he know he isn't in love with you? Charlotte, nothing is to be gained by allowing him to slip out of the sacred bonds of marriage without a major confrontation and conflict. He tells you to keep the house, get an attorney to settle on your terms, and he will agree to any reasonable proposition you make. He wants an easy exit. It won't work. He won't learn anything from the experience, and you'll be left with mammoth rage and feelings of degradation that have nowhere to go but against yourself. Neither of you will grow from the experience. Your souls could be wounded for the rest of your lives.

So, my dear Charlotte, persevere. Let's define the problem regardless of what we do with it. In today's world I do not think two responsible persons have the right to walk away from a marriage without first submitting themselves to the insight and guidance of some form of psychotherapy. Before you do anything, use whatever leverage you possess to persuade Bud to enter therapy. Then, let's see where we go from there.

My heart is leaden with the awful weight of your shock and pain. Don't do anything drastic, my dear. Count on me to be with you each step of the way—physically and prayerfully.

With my love,

$\int$ ←

Dear Bud,

Thank you for your phone call. Of course, I would be happy to see you any time. You know I stand ready to help in any possible way you might deem to be useful.

However, the distance between us makes any assistance in depth impractical, and therefore I earnestly urge you to accept Charlotte's plea that you both agree to see the therapist I have recommended. He is highly skilled. I have made many referrals to him over the years, and although his batting average is not perfect, it comes close to it. What more could we ask? You have both put fourteen valuable years into this marriage. It deserves every break you can give it.

I'm glad Charlotte showed you my letter. I continue to be completely bewildered by your decision. As I told Charlotte, there wasn't a shred of conflict that prepared me for such an action. If there was one marriage I would have predicted to be permanent, it was yours.

Of course, I'm grateful and honored if you want to make the trip to visit me, as you say, "to explain the situation."

I look forward to next Friday afternoon to see your good and cherished face again.

With loving regard,

Tom

Dear Charlotte,

We both now know the facts. Both of us also had a sick suspicion about the truth, but we didn't dare allow ourselves to face it until Bud found the courage to provide us with the denouement of the plot. I'm sure we both understand why he told me about his situation first.

I believe he is sincere, Charlotte, when he tells us that he wanted to protect you. Bud is still Bud. I know it is hard for you to trust anything he says to you these days. At your core you have every right to feel enraged and betrayed. Yet, Bud is not normally a man lacking in integrity and responsibility, nor is he now. He believed he could follow the scenario he had planned, and I feel sure he thought he could do it. It is typical of him to think he could accomplish anything he set his mind on doing. Some of that naive confidence comes from his lack of insight, and some of it comes from the fact that he is usually successful in carrying out anything he wants to do. He sincerely thought he could walk away from his marriage, conceal his involvement with Elizabeth and remarry at a time that would leave you as unwounded as possible, and keep his own reputation intact. What he didn't count on was the intensity of your reaction, and the inescapable integrity of his own heart, when faced with the fire of your truth and love. That's why he avoided a face-to-face encounter with you until you took matters into your own hands and forced a confrontation. I hope you don't feel guilty about having used the aid of friends and a strategy of subterfuge to have pulled that one off. He left you with no choice.

When he came to see me and told me about Elizabeth, I begged him not to make any commitment about his future. I pled with him to move back into your home. I appealed to him as a professional person to give therapy an opportunity to redefine your marriage. I reminded him that he had made referrals in similar situations himself. I told him he would have to sacrifice his relation to Elizabeth until he was at least on the other side of the mountain of therapy. I promised him I would say nothing to you about his situation because I fully recognized that to be his responsibility, and only his responsibility.

He was furious with me. It wasn't an open hostility with name calling and guilty defenses, but throughout the second hour of the visit I could feel the vibrations of his seething resentment at my directness with him. After he left I thought, He thinks he can get away with it on his terms, and maybe he can. I temporarily forgot about the steel in your fibre.

I'm not surprised about his refusal to see a therapist. When he was here with me, he gave perfunctory recognition to my words about therapy, but I knew then it was a polite but negative response. He thinks he knows as much as a psychiatrist does about these things, which of course misses the point. Bud is always someone who has overintellectualized his emotions, and there lies the key to the problem.

Don't let him off the hook, Charlotte. Although he refuses to go the route I have begged him to take, at least he has consented to a series of meetings with you. Neither of you are inarticulate persons nor ignorant of the complexities of motivation. Stick to him like a fly to flypaper until you have spelled out together, as best you can, why and how this all happened. You owe it to yourself. You can be sure he will repeat the pattern if he doesn't learn something about himself through this experience. He doesn't want the pain of that exercise, but, dear Charlotte, there's no way around it, and in your heart I think you agree with me that Bud is still Bud, a person in whom you and I have seen, and will see again, qualities of greatness. You surely deserve a life far, far better than he now gives you, but he does, too. For his soul's sake, I pray he finds it through the inevitable pain you are both enduring.

Keep in touch. Remember I'm here when you need me.

Much love,

J.

Dear Charlotte,

What would we do without the telephone and our infrequent visits? I agree with your decision to terminate therapy. It has served you well for the past year. I knew you would find that man vastly supportive, and I thank God he helped to preserve your essential self from falling apart. You are still quite fragile, but there is a healthiness in your spirit that now has the upper hand and your "faith will make you whole."

There are two things I want to touch on as your spiritual director that need your strenuous effort, but before I do I want to share with you some thoughts about being in love that I have been pondering of late. I tried to get Bud to think along these lines when I saw him a few weeks ago, just after the divorce settlement was signed. I made no progress at all, but I left him a book entitled *We* by Paul Johnson. So often, the only way to reach Bud is through the mind. Maybe he will read it, but I wouldn't be surprised if he gives it a heave-ho after the first fifty pages.

The appalling power of the in love experience was never more vividly brought home to me than it was in your experience with Bud. You are a handsome woman of gaiety and warmth with many gifts. You are fun to be with. Your tastes and interests are sophisticated. You are forty-one, an age that for divorced women is a lot luckier than fifty-one. Men are easily drawn to you. All of this is by way of saying, Charlotte, that I strongly covet for you a new experience of falling in love. What I have to say about the experience is not to demean it nor to fail to rejoice in it. You will not heal quickly after the trauma of your divorce. Your emotions run too deeply for that to happen. Yet I eagerly await the day when you call to tell me you have met someone very, very special and want me to meet him. I long for that call when your voice will tell me you are in love.

So you see, Charlotte, it isn't that I don't value the experience of being in love, or that I don't prize all it means to me. I would be the worst of ingrates if I did not acknowledge the treasures of being in love, and all it has given to me.

Yet, I have come to see that most of us invest the

experience of falling in love with a quality of transcendence that really belongs to the province of religion. It is evident in the way we talk about it. We give to the ecstasy of love the language of religious devotion. Bud told me he felt more alive, fulfilled, at peace with himself, than he had ever felt in his life. His countenance took on a spiritual radiance when he spoke of Elizabeth. "I adore her," he told me. "She is worth any sacrifice I have to make. She has given my life new meaning and purpose. I have a confidence in myself I never had before. I worship the ground she walks on."

Charlotte, my dear, it is difficult for me to write to you about Bud. Yet, you have come far since the initial trauma of his departure. Like most of us, you are one who has to understand a problem before you can move on to solve it. Once your mental fingers grasp some tools by which you can deal with thorny issues, you always make progress.

Let me explain. As you know, Bud used to make jokes with me about being a "Christmas and Easter Christian." He clearly believed in the importance of the church as an institutional support of civilized society, and therefore his financial contribution was significant; but as far as his spiritual needs were concerned, it was enough for him to attend Christmas Eve services and enjoy the candles and the carols. Also, he wasn't all that fond of Easter sermons; but he thought he owed it to tradition to be in church on Easter, and besides that, he would say to me, "The flowers are nice."

Now, Charlotte, you and I know that Bud is a guy with remarkable gifts of compassion and perception. There are few people I'd rather spend an evening with talking about the issues and problems of our time. He is a great person of many parts, but there is one large area of his life he has never recognized.

I remember one evening you and I were talking about how important the Eucharist is to both of us. Bud was about to use the word "cannibalistic" in dismissing our depth of reverence for the Holy Communion. He stopped himself and said with that shy smile of his, "You guys are out of my depth. I'll keep my mouth shut." I think there was a corner of his heart that wanted to share your religious faith. He saw what serenity and humility it gave you. I never heard him disparage it, or ever discourage you from all those wonderful things you do through the church to reach out to the community's neediest people. I think he always knew that prayer and worship were at the center of the person you are, but I doubt if he ever once seriously thought those things might be crucial for his growth.

My point, Charlotte, is that Bud was vulnerable to the ecstasy of falling in love again in part because he had no place in his life for the energies of worship, adoration, inner quietude, and spiritual development. That may seem farfetched to you, but I have become convinced that when we deny ourselves any space for the spirit of the Living God, we are driven to fill our hunger for experience of the transcendent with some pseudoreligion. For millions of Americans pseudoreligion is falling in love, as well as a hundred other things we could easily name.

If Bud had been willing to open himself a few years ago to spiritual reality, and even a fraction of its disciplines, I question whether he would have considered divorce as a possibility. I don't mean that in any moralistic sense. Bud is far from ever becoming an immoral person. That is not the issue.

I am talking about the thirst for ecstasy that is innate to human nature. We all crave to be carried out of ourselves by that which transcends ourselves. You and I have come to see how the Eucharist, penance, forgiveness, inner quietude, celebrations that integrate the Christ Event into our own life stories, praise, and obedience nourish our experience of the Holy Presence.

The times of ecstasy when, for a sacred moment, we are lifted out of ourselves into another dimension of awesome sorrow or joy in God's love are rare. You will remember what happened to me at the Good Friday evening service as I was reflecting on the words of Christ, "My God, my God, why hast thou forsaken me?" It was an instant when the sorrow of Christ for the forsaken in this world and my own poor mirror of that sorrow became one. I'll never forget that moment, nor will you, Charlotte, because you entered its depth with me. Those times are ever so rare, but they wouldn't happen to us at all if we didn't open ourselves to the possibility of transendence with some humble regularity. In the meantime, we are nourished. The bread of life keeps us alive, and we grow in grace.

I am not sure the rituals and rites, the liturgies, and submission to spiritual direction that we prize would ever be acceptable to Bud. God knows our way doesn't fit everyone. No human being, no institution, no creed, no liturgy, can limit the freedom of God. Divine love finds ways to reach all of us if we are but serious about the search. I believe that if Bud ever took up the search out of a real recognition of his spiritual needs, he would find his own path to spiritual reality, and it would be different from our path.

In the meantime, he has fallen in love again, and that fills all his needs to adore and to be made whole. I wonder what will happen to him fourteen years from now. Will his hunger for ecstasy be kindled again by a new liaison? I doubt it. He'll be in his late fifties then, and I pray he will have learned how real love can be for two people who grow together with reverence for each other's space, cherishing each other in tenderness and respect, sharing the burdens and the joys of life, not in ecstatic bliss but in mutual steadfast responsibility and openness, grateful to God for the capacity to forgive and to be forgiven, day by day, year by year.

I have spent so much time on this aspect of Bud's journey, Charlotte, because I really think it is at the essence of why this all happened. Oh, I know you and your therapist thought maybe you were too strong, too overcontrolling, that you made too many of the important decisions, that when he ceased to need your strengths he looked to someone of the clinging vine ilk. I take all of that *cum grano*. You and I have acknowledged that there may be a crumb of validity in those insights, but not enough to break up a marriage that had as much mutual satisfaction in it at every level as yours possessed. The roots of the problem lie much more in Bud's overintellectualizing of his emotions before he allows himself to feel, and in the starvation of his spiritual life. He was ripe for an experience of shattering emotional power, and the culture we live in set him up for it.

Now, as your spiritual director there are two directions in which I ask you to concentrate your inward energies in the immediate future. They are connected, but they are two separate steps.

The first is to begin the labor of forgiveness. You won't be free to continue your soul's journey until you can sincerely forgive Bud. Your resentments, jealousies, vengeful plots, outrage, have been given full and justified expression in your journal, with your therapist, and with me. I have admired beyond measure the way in which you have maintained your distance about it with everyone else. I guess that's a part of your natural reserve and privacy. However, do you not think the time has come to release Bud, to surrender your need to hurt him and denigrate him? I believe you are drawing near to that time, and I ask you to consider it. If you are not, tell me, and we will wait for the fruit of release to ripen. When you are ready to begin this labor, let me know, and I will tell you how we begin.

In the meantime, please use whatever you learned in therapy about remembering your dreams. Write them down. Naturally, it is not my purpose to use them as a therapist, but they will be enormously helpful to me in guiding us to know how ready you are to undertake the work of forgiveness and what kind of real progress we are making with it when we do tackle the issue.

The second request I want to make of you is also painful, and again it depends on your readiness. Don't undertake this one, either, if you feel it is beyond your powers at this time. When last I was in your home you showed me drawers full of envelopes containing scores of photographs you and Bud took of one another and of your travels. I want you to purchase some large albums and organize the pictures chronologically. Then I want you to paste them seriatim in the albums.

Those photos represent more than fourteen years of your life. Everything they represent must be reassimilated through the veil of the divorce trauma. You will weep, but eventually you will also laugh. That exercise in memory will be the prelude to relinquishment. You can't say good-bye to those years with a sweep of the hand. You have to live through them again, sift them, and measure them. When you have finished, you will be left with a new strength in your soul. You will experience the joy and love you gave to those years. You will come out of the experience with regrets, maybe some remorse, but with a new confidence in yourself. You may even say to yourself, "Well, Charlotte, you weren't so bad after all! Poor Bud, he doesn't know how much he has lost."

Peace and love, my dear,

Joe +

My dear Janet,

You sat in your car at the foot of my driveway until 2:00 or 3:00 A.M. I don't know when you left because I finally gave up and fell into a fitful sleep.

Your silences and your pain not only frighten me, Janet, but also infuriate me. We have gone through this routine so many times. After pleading with you to tell me what I could do to help, I ran out of patience. For two hours we sat together in your car while I begged you to talk and to share your anguish with me. At least half of the time you cried silently while I sat immobilized and helpless. Nothing seemed to touch the source of your pain. Not even a threat of emergency medical assistance or police intervention made any impression on you.

I hope you understood my exhaustion when I left your car and went into the house. Holly, my daughter, asked me, "Why won't she come in the house and sleep in the guest room?" My honest reply was "I don't know." Somewhere around dawn I got up and looked out the window. There was enough light in the sky to see the street clearly. Your car was gone. I wondered when you had left. Then the thought came to me that you might have departed shortly after you saw the last light in our house turned off. There was nothing more you could do. The end of the line for the night had been reached. You knew it, and drove home.

I have tried long and hard to understand you. Believe me, Janet, there is nothing I wouldn't do to help you. How many years has it been since you heard me give a series of lectures at that conference in Wisconsin? It was the next summer at a similar conference that we met again. Your move to Philadelphia subsequently enabled us to begin our agonizing search for wholeness.

Is there a single path we have failed to pursue in our quest? I am staggered by the volume of our effort in every conceivable direction.

Your tentative faith in God's healing power has been my great hope. Do you remember how excited I was when Agnes Sanford agreed to come to our church to conduct a healing mission? It was in 1959 that she and I began a friendship that blessed me immeasurably for almost a quarter of a century until her recent death in California. I used to share in the leadership of her conferences on healing prayer and pastoral care. Her talks, her books, above all, her spirit, taught me more about expectant faith and trustful intercession than anyone in my whole life. People write about these things today as though they had just discovered gold in Alaska, when in fact Agnes was giving us the same insights in the 1940s and the 1950s.

She prayed for you that first evening in my study at that mission. You and I were in our first year of serious effort to overcome your monstrous depressions. Our friendship had barely begun. Agnes told both of us to be perfectly quiet for a period of preparation. We had told her a little of your life story and of our goals. She stood behind the chair in which you were sitting, for what seemed an interminable period of time. As the silence prevailed, I was puzzled. Yet it didn't occur to me to interrupt the quietness. I could see that Agnes was in agony of the spirit. She was perspiring. Her eyes were squeezed shut in a prolonged mystery of concentration.

Finally, she walked around from the back of the chair and sat down on the sofa beside me. She looked at both of us with a strange expression. "Janet," she said, "I'm afraid there's nothing I can do for you at this time. Jesus has told me, 'This kind can come out only by much prayer and fasting.' You and Joe will have to persevere in your task a long time. My spirit can not see far enough to perceive the end." Then she brusquely asked if she could be alone and we were both dismissed. I was stunned. You were a crumpled mass of tears.

Today I understand a little more of what was going on in my study that night. At the time I resolved my stunned puzzlement by an unyielding faith in Agnes. I didn't doubt for a moment that she knew what she was doing and that at some future date I would understand what it was all about. Beyond question, she discerned something highly relevant to our problem. Clearly, she did not feel it wise to discuss it with us. After some reflection later that evening, I was content to let the matter rest on Agnes's wisdom.

Janet, you and I have both wondered if you could be held in the power of an alien spirit. You came to the conclusion long before I did that you are often possessed by a compelling will separate from your own. Some overmastering urge pushes you to distort the truth for your own purposes, to destroy someone's reputation, or to alienate a friendship through excessive misrepresentation. You are fantastically clever and resourceful in polarizing people. I tremble with fear when I hear you speak highly of someone, because I know it will not be long before you have found a flaw in their character that you can use to denigrate them. Sometimes you do it with consummate subtlety, and sometimes it's more like a sledgehammer.

For years I held to the belief that this destructive pattern had an adequate explanation in the complicated forest of your past emotional history. Psychotherapy would show you a path out of the wilderness, and I think it has; but the thing hasn't worked. You've been helped, but not healed, at least, not until now!

As I look back on the convoluted windings of your destructiveness, I realize I wouldn't believe it if I hadn't seen it. What is it about you that draws severe storms to your soul's terrain? Nothing is ever calm or serene for you for more than a brief season. You seem to thrive on issues of fearful gravity. When I first knew you, a third marriage was waiting in the wings. Although you had set the date and made the arrangements for a huge reception, my intuition told me the thing was never going to come off. Happiness appears to be unendurable for you.

I guess I'll never know why you broke off that wedding. Ed seemed like the right man for you. Whereas you are volatile, he is steady. Your irrational actions are balanced by his careful judgment. Your all-over-the-place affections are contained by his quiet reserve. Your murderous depressions are ameliorated by his even-handed temperament and good sense.

What was it that made you track down Ed's former wife? You didn't learn anything you didn't previously know. Her stories of his alcoholism and violence were well known. Ed told you about his past as fully as anyone could reasonably expect. I'm not even sure your account of his physical abuse of his first wife is true. He told you Lorraine had grossly exaggerated it. Why did you insist on belaboring the incident until it poisoned everything? You knew, didn't you, that if you accused Ed of prevarication and of being a Dr. Jekyll and Mr. Hyde sufficiently, you would push him right out of the wedding. Not one of us who was there that day will forget the nastiness of the scene. I think we knew after the first five minutes that the wedding was off, and I think Ed knew it too, though he tried every approach imaginable to get you to put the issue down.

It's all endlessly complex, isn't it, Janet? I think it is useless to ask questions that imply a large margin of choice. We gain nothing by implying that you could have done something quite different from that which you did. It is helpful only if you ask the questions of yourself in search of the underlying causes in you own inheritance and life story. Understanding is a priceless pearl, but sometimes we have to admit that it is buried so deeply in the mire of the past that it is unavailable to us. As you and I have wept and strained to widen our comprehension of your problems, I have often come to the conclusion that the solution is really beyond our reach. It isn't a question of being unwilling to change. You want to be free of many of your compulsions. I don't doubt that, but your will alone is inadequate to the task.

After you married Charlie, I had high hopes that his jovial, loving nature would give your life some new hope. He was such a nice guy. We all liked being around him. His jokes were dated and repetitive, but his nature was so free of malice we all enjoyed him and loved him. It serves no purpose to ask why you resurrected an old liaison with Tom, your second husband. I don't think you know why. You tell me that sex with Tom is the best you've every had and that Charlie was pretty inadequate in that department.

But, Janet, I don't buy that explanation. Every man who comes into your life gets hurt. You find ways to betray his love or to alienate him. Your demands are appalling. Insatiability is a mild word to describe your needs in an intimate relationship.

Do you remember Dr. Draper? Was he the second or the third psychiatrist I persuaded you to see? His approach to your problems was far from gentle, and although he used a meat cleaver on you psyche, I think you'll agree he helped more than any of the others we consulted. Remember his remark at the end of your third interview? "God, but you are one hell of a bore." Nor have I forgotten how you ruefully agreed with him when he said to me, "She'll suck and suck and suck, until you're dry and withered, then she'll throw you away and find a new teat to suck."

I've wondered, Janet, what would have happened to you if you hadn't inherited so much money. It's a vain line of thought to pursue because your soul's condition is inseparable from your family history, but I've often thought about the camel in the eye of the needle when thinking

about the evil consequences of your money. You have had
options most of us will never have. Your wealth and your
style have drawn people and things to you that have kept
the temperature of your psyche at an unabated and fevered
pitch.

Isn't it strange how extremes produce extremes? Those
who have grossly too little in early life, and those who have
grossly too much in early life, frequently end up with the
same compulsions. Nothing is ever enough. They are driven
to seek more, ever more; more things, more love, more
money, more assurance, more symbols of fulfillment, and
more proof of devotion. *The Guiness Book of Records* isn't
large enough to tabulate their wants.

You suffered from both extremities, Janet. Fearing you
would want too many things, your parents raised you as
though they couldn't afford to buy you more than the
essentials. Report card time was always a time when your
father reminded you how much it was costing him to send
you to a private school. Both parents were so enmeshed in
the coils of their own deceits and ambitions that they had
little if any emotional energy left to recognize who you
were or what you were asking. They, too, suffered from the
extremities of deprivation and need.

You have frequently confessed to me, with a bitter
smile, that you "use people." That's both true and untrue.
When I have asked why you say that, your response is
"That's what my friends tell me when they cut me off."
Janet, we all use one another. Interdependence is universal. I
am a debtor to a host of people whom I have used. There
isn't a chapter in my journey that fails to record how
grateful I am to people who helped me on the way: with my

education, with my crisis experiences of development as a child, as an adolescent, in my war experience, with my marriage, with my spiritual consciousness and growth. It goes on to the present hour. I have taken what these people in their generosity have given me, and gratefully used it. I hope I have returned to others some meagre measure of all I have received.

Don't use you own guilt and the negative judgments of others to prevent you from seeing your positive side. You have been more blessed than you will allow yourself to believe, and you have blessed others more generously than you will permit yourself to see. You have never closed your door on a friend in desperate need. You have helped dozens of causes and numberless people anonymously, with no expectation of return or recognition.

Of course, there is the other side. You have used your sex, your sensuousness, your money and the freedom it gives you, your social status, your charitable contributions, your close friendships with both sexes, as a way of compelling life to revolve around you with rapt attention and admiration. The paradox of all this activity is that it leaves you as empty as a pumpkin shell with no candle in it. And so you sit in your car at the foot of my driveway, speechless and suicidal.

It may seem ludicrous for me to say that we have come to a time of blessedness. I wish I knew why this certainty is so unshakable in me. There is a new creature forming in you. A spirit of evil destruction has left you.

It didn't grasp me as an undeniable truth until this morning. Last night was so fuzzy and anxiety producing that it all merged into one blur of confusion in my mind. It was about 9:30. I was sitting meditatively in my study, holding you in the presence of the healing Christ. Then it came to me! We walked together out of the wilderness last night! I'm sure it's true. We were sitting silently in your car. You made no response by gesture or sound to my pleadings. I reached and took both of your cold, clammy hands into my own. A buzzing in my ears made me aware of the intensity of the moment. I felt as though we were in the center of a powerful outburst of magnetic electrical energy. I can't remember the exact words. I prayed, "Blessed and Holy Healer, Saviour of Janet and of me, I beg you to deliver Janet from the father of lies. May the prince of darkness and confusion have no more power over her. Unleash her from the bondage of this evil spirit and set her free to be your daughter, the person you made her to be in your sight. I claim it in your name and offer you our unending thanks and glory and praise." You began to weep after that. About an hour later I left you in your car, deeply perplexed.

This morning I am seized by a conviction that it has happened, Janet. Many things have prepared the way for this moment: your experiences of psychotherapy, good and bad; your own native goodness and intelligence; our consultations; our prayers; all those dozens of times when I have laid my hands on your head and claimed healing, release, forgiveness—all these together and more, Janet, have given us this moment.

There is now a new emptiness in you. It is not the old absence of love or trust or hope. It is more like a crucible that has been washed clean, glistening white, waiting to be filled by God's goodness. I know it is true, dear Janet. Please don't resist grace. We are at one of those watershed moments in the journey of the soul.

God comes to us with life-changing power, not through reason but through the heart. I do not need God to explain the laws of his universe to me or to fulfill my consuming desire to reconcile his loving power with the ubiquitous enormity of suffering and evil. The Almighty is neither opposed to reason nor can there be a contradiction between truth and God. Yet I have learned to live with the text "Verily thou art a god who hidest thyself." Nevertheless, we do not find God; it is God who finds us.

Our souls are frail barks on the stormy sea of destiny. When the tempest reaches a high pitch we come to our senses and the sleeping Christ awakens within us. He is stirred by our urgent cries. At once he comes to the surface of consciousness and brings peace to the troubled waters. The surprise of grace is that he has been slumberously waiting all the while for us to rouse him.

Janet, the Christ within you rose to the surface of your soul last night. He is calling you to himself in holy love. For too long you have thought of yourself as unloved, unworthy, and unfaithful. You have tried to prove to the world that you are all of that, but the patient Christ is not to be mocked. He has patiently waited until all else failed. Your cries arose from such a depth of sincerity and integrity last night that the moment of grace was at hand. A new birth was aborning.

I can remember as a child standing before a mirror staring at myself. Like all children, I made many silly and exaggerated faces at myself. Then I stopped. I remember asking a deadly serious question, "Who are you?" I inquired. "Who are you?" The question had no answer. I only felt an abyss of yawning, frightening emptiness. Was I the person in the mirror, or was I someone else no mirror could reflect? I ran frantically from the room and busily engaged myself in some activity that would dispel the fear of the vision.

That night my mother read to me, as was her wont, from Hurlburt's *Story of the Bible*. She read about the widow of Nain and how Jesus had compassion for her grief. The child in the coffin was her only son. When mother read how Jesus raised the boy from the dead, I knew in some vague unnameable sense I had myself been raised from the abyss of nothingness. I was my mother's youngest child and I belonged to Jesus. It was as simple as that. I would never forget again who I was!

A story of the poet Rilke's childhood experience comes to my mind. He had been rummaging in the attic. He found a huge, fearsome costume. He put it on. He stared at his image through the awful mask that covered his face. He felt himself sinking, lost in a bottomless pit. In panic he tried to get out of the costume, but it was useless. The harder he tried, the more entangled he became in the wretched thing. Finally, he tumbled down the stairway. His cries were heard. The servants laughed at his antics and pleas until one of them recognized the pain in his voice and released him from his terror.

Janet, I want you to receive the Eucharist every morning at the first communion in the cathedral for the next two weeks. Each morning, hold that bread in your hand and welcome the chalice of wine to your lips as signs of Christ's awakened presence in your soul, calling you to himself as his very own, belonging to him, filled by him, forgiven by him, blessed by him. Do not offend him by refusing his love because of some sick feeling that you are unworthy of his mercy. He knows this moment of grace pulses with the beat of new faith and hope in you. He has set you free from the frightening mask you have worn all these years. Don't, I beseech you, don't refuse him. It is a beginning; it is the most important beginning of your life.

The walk of faith is never reduced to neat, pious assurances by the great saints and mystics of the church. They all warn us to be careful of horrendous letdowns after the high moments of commitment have come. So, Janet, don't be surprised if in the next two weeks it seems like arduous, impossible mountain climbing, but, my dear, I know you have experienced the personal presence of the Holy Spirit. Why it happened now and not yesterday, this year instead of last year, at this late stage of your life instead of an earlier stage before so much was wasted and so much pain given and received, I don't know. We either experience him personally, or we don't. We either know he is with us and among us and within us, or we don't. The timing belongs to the wisdom and inscrutable mystery of God.

All I can say is that God is the consciousness of the universe, and you are now among those who have come into an inward undeniable awareness of the cord that binds your consciousness through the Christ of the Gospels to the

God of creation, from eternity to eternity. I am absolutely
on tiptoe after all these years of mutual effort to know what
God is going to do with you now!

With my love,

Joe

*[P.S. to the reader: It is true! Janet has been set free. Today,
some time later, she is among the most responsible and
caring Christians I know.]*

My dear Jack,

This is an unbelievably difficult letter for me to write. There are several reasons I have put off doing it. One is that we have cared about each other for more than forty years, and it is presumptuous of me to think I might have anything to say to someone who is more experienced in life than I am. Yet, you have asked me a question that involves matters of imperative magnitude. I am bound to attempt an answer. It is also not easy for me because your question raises issues I have suffered with myself. If I am to reply in any way that reaches the center of the problem, I shall have to deal in unvarnished truths. I fear the risk of misunderstanding. The last thing I want to do is to alienate a prized friendship.

Ever since your beloved Hilary died, I have sensed a change in you. Her death and the precariousness of your present health have clearly precipitated a crisis. Each time I have seen you, the subject of death has come up. You joke about it. You say, "Well, if anyone can make it, I'm sure Hilary did," or you say, "The evidence is all against you, Joe." I ask, "What are you talking about?" and you say, "Survival beyond the grave."

Now comes this letter from you. Clearly, your religious training and church attendance, however much you decry them, deposited some seeds of faith along the way. Otherwise you would not write, ''I just don't know what to think about the next life, but for safety's sake I feel the need to clean up my act. You know me better than anyone except Hilary. When I was more than my usual obnoxious self she would say, 'Jack, why don't you do something about your everlasting self-centeredness? Sometimes you really embarrass me. You can't talk about anything except as it relates to you.' I always knew she was right. I *am* a bore, but I never did anything about it and now I'd like to. Will you help me?''

Jack, I have never had someone seventy-three years old, facing the end of his life, ask me a question about himself that carries as much gravity and meaning as you have done. It is typical of you. Probably it is related to your training in the legal profession. When you step out of yourself and apply your considerable mental abilities to any given problem, you have a way of zinging in on the target.

You have used Hilary's word ''self-centeredness.'' Obviously, the word has a valuable coinage in general conversation, but I dislike it because it carries a weight of self-righteous judgment. I would rather think of it as the problem of a wounded ego. It is no simple issue. The numbers of us who have suffered the consequences of wounded egos are legion. The depth of the problem is prodigiously complex. Please bear with me as I struggle to spell it out.

In the writings of a great mystic of India whose thought I have valued many years, I found an image that has helped me to understand our inner divisions. I have taken his image and interpreted it for the purposes of this letter. He compares each of us to a seventeenth-century equipage. Imagine a shining black coach with a coat of arms emblazoned on the doors. The coachman sits on his tall perch overlooking the horses in their gleaming harnesses. The reins are held loosely in his hands. He proudly wears a high silk top hat. Within the coach there sits a solitary figure—silent, serene, patient. He gives no orders. He waits.

The coach symbolizes our identity as physical beings. The coachman represents the power of the ego. The horses are the images of our emotional drives. The figure in the coach is the Christ, the Master, the Soul Maker, waiting until his presence is recognized or until the coach is mired in a frightening ditch and his help is urgently required.

Sometimes the coach is in a miserable condition. The wheels won't turn. The suspension is out of balance. The window won't open. The interior is an unspeakable mess.

Usually, the coachman is so full of himself that he assumes he is in charge of all he so proudly surveys from his high perch in the world. This is often a pose, because there are numberless occasions when his livery is soiled, his hat is blown off his head by a sudden gust of wind, or his hands shake and falter as he reaches for the horses' whip at his side.

Nor can we forget how from time to time the horses are docile and obedient, responsive to the slightest tug of the bit in their mouths. There are many unexpected occasions when something arouses them, some fear takes hold of them, some passion seizes them, and the entire equipage is in serious jeopardy.

In all these conditions, the soul maker waits. No storm, no accident, no peril, no neglect, no forgetfulness, no rejection, causes him to leave the coach. He simply is waiting with boundless courtesy to be invited to participate in the journey. He yearns with infinite intensity to be asked to bring harmony and order to the various needs of the coach, the coachman, and the horses. At various stages of the journey, there are way stations, places of pause or places of crisis. It is there that the Master looks eagerly from the windows, hoping against hope that now he will be given attention and reverence so that all the different parts can be fashioned into a performance of wholeness, each part-functioning in harmony with each other part.

Alas, all too often the soul maker is forgotten and the way station is nothing more than a watering trough. Never mind, the Master thinks, ''I'll wait for the next one.

There are also crises of horrendous proportions when the entire equipage is in severe danger. The soul maker rises. He beats on the roof for attention. He shouts. He warns. He pleads. The crisis may be overcome and order restored, the crisis may be a prelude to the beginning of irreversible damage, or the crisis may not be overcome. Then come disintegration and death.

When I ponder your life, I think the source of the misery you have experienced, Jack, is an early wound to your confidence in yourself as a person. You suffered grievously and consistently from lack of respect and provision for your right to be the person you are. There wasn't enough security in your family to go around. You were forgotten in the crowd. You were preceded by two brothers and two sisters and you were followed by more siblings. The death of your mother as you were entering those destiny-forming years of adolescence took the anger and neglect and confusion of your earlier years and transposed them into a key of unbearable intensity. By the time you were eighteen, a pattern of insecurity and rebellion was fixed. The pain of those wounds compelled the ego in you to act out incredible feats of defense and concealment. There was an endless confusion in you between the world of reality and the world of fantasy. Between the bleeding, overly-defensive coachman and the wild team of horses at your command, you were driven to excesses of every kind, including long and threatening addictions. The equipage never knew where it was going. The zigzags were countless.

Meanwhile, the Master within was seldom heard or recognized. His presence could not be banished, but he could be ignored. Several times when you were hospitalized as a result of your various accidents, the Christ within tried valiantly to obtain your attention, but you were largely deaf to his voice. How could it have been otherwise, considering the fact that you were never seriously opened to the potential blessedness he intends for all of us?

After that dreadful accident twenty-seven years ago, I'll never forget seeing you at Boston City Hospital. It was hard to find you in that oxygen tent, with your left leg elevated and your head bandaged beyond recognition. The coach was almost destroyed.

When you were beginning to recover, you told me that two things seemed miraculous to you: the first was that you had, ten minutes before the accident, left your companion at her door, and the second was that there was no one behind you or in the opposite lane to pile on top of you as you careened across that busy highway, wholly out of control. I had previously been struck by the fact that when you smashed up a car, or injured yourself, you were consistently alone!

You know, surely, how grateful we were that this accident made you admit yourself to a hospital for treatment of alcoholism and join the AA program, which has kept you sober for twenty-seven years.

I am convinced that the Master within reached you faintly but with sufficient instinctive power to make sure you were alone when you endangered your life. I believe, too, it was that divine impulse from your depths that somehow knew, in that accident, that if you were going to crash there was a single best moment to do it. And what do you think it is that keeps you in AA all these years?

Let's come back to the coachman and the horses. Jack, your ego needs and your emotional needs have held you in bondage all your life. You are a driven man. The coachman has been the slave of the horses, and the horses have been the slaves of the coachman. The value of every relation, of every experience, pivots around your excessive need for approval, recognition, fulfillment, satisfaction, power, ego-support. Your fundamental absence of respect for yourself compels you to seek it with insatiable greed from others. Your suspicion that you are at bottom a selfish, no-good guy drives you to require the opposite feedback from all the sources you can command or con into serving the needs of your ego. Your certainty that you are not worthy to be loved plays havoc with the people who love you, because there is no end to your demands that they prove their love to you. Your sexual conquests are connected to those demands. The clever, ingenious, and obvious ways in which you manipulate us are tests to see if we will stand by you or desert you in spite of your nastiness and betrayals.

Much of your addiction to alcohol grew out of that wounded ego. Hilary's greatness was that her total commitment to you in love broke the shell of your pretenses and for almost the first time in your experience the horses of your nature felt a rein of authority in their mouths. They were susceptible to new direction. Rather than lose the hope of marriage to Hilary, you were willing to commit yourself to treatment for your addiction. You pushed her to the very brink, you will remember. I confess I, too, thought you had lost her; but that dreadful accident brought her back, and beyond a doubt, things have been different ever since.

But the wounded ego is still there, demanding excessive attention, pushing you, even at seventy-three, into a fantasy world of new plans accomplished, added wealth achieved, or noble generosity extended that would yield a harvest of appreciation and admiration.

Remember when Hilary forgot your seventy-first birthday? You behaved like a rejected infant, although her illness was uppermost in all our minds. It wasn't your fault, Jack. The last thing I want to do is to start that guilty nerve of yours vibrating. That's the easiest thing in the world to do. We do it to one another in the most diabolical and consistent ways!

No, dear friend, it is not guilt I am after, but truth. Guilt enslaves; truth liberates. That precious ego of yours was never nourished with the qualities of respect and reverence, which are the heritage of every human being. You never received the measure of personal nurturance your nature required. It wasn't your fault that it was so, nor that of your parents. They had their own inner battles and insecurities to deal with. That was just the way it was. I don't begin to fathom the mystery of fate, or "karma" as they call it in the East. Sooner or later we have to accept the things we cannot change. He who does not make peace with his destiny will rue the day he failed to do so. None of us is given the privilege of deciding the time or period in which we are born. Nor can we choose the home in which we shall be raised. Nor can we determine who our parents shall be. That's the way it is, and evermore shall be.

In China a child is not named until twenty-eight days after the child's birth. The naming day is synchronized with the mysterious bond between the moon and the tide, the rhythm of blood and nature. On that day the eldest member of the family takes the child on his or her knees. The child becomes calm. The elder "parent" looks long and penetratingly upon the child's face. Fingers carefully caress the shape of the child's face, especially the eyebrows and cheekbones. Then out of the breathless silence of those participating in the ritual, the child is named. In your case, the words would have been "Your name is John." It is said that a perceptible difference in the child's behavior can be seen after the naming ceremony.

I cherish that scene. It is an affirmation of the wonder of personhood. It suggests a reverence for the uniqueness of each individual. It bespeaks the mystery of our being. It represents a dimension of reverence I wish every one of us were given from birth.

Alas, Jack, you were denied that affirmation. You have suffered from its wounded consequences for seventy-three years. It simply wasn't in the cards. The family constellation, the realities, the unavoidable neuroses surrounding your growing up, made it impossible.

It is no surprise that you did everything in your power to deny your lot. You entered a world of fantasy and make-believe as an adolescent. You created myths of family history and achievement that had little, if any, basis in fact. You took on the identity of anyone who commanded your admiration and envy. Lacking any sense of your own value as a person, you sought the value of others.

Your great concession to the facts of your situation was your determination to succeed intellectually. Your academic progress was nothing if not spectacular. You knew education would open doors of self-affirmation for you, although you had a confused notion of who you were. Once you were established professionally, you knew your future economic security was assured. Your experience in law school and in that stellar clerkship you had in Washington gave you opportunities not many of your classmates could match.

After you were settled in the firm, you had energy left over for more rebellion, and how you rebelled! At least you had style. It will serve no purpose to review those years of alcoholism, marriage, parenting, divorce, and then Hilary. You have replayed them to yourself in guilty dreams too often already.

My one comfort is that following your marriage to Hilary, and after sobriety, there were countless times of deep satisfaction and joy in your succeeding years, although your wounded ego made you limp through them always compelled to defend yourself, forever drawing attention to your past, your achievements, your experience.

You couldn't help it, Jack. The outer appearance of the coachman was, as ever, of supreme importance to you. In the past twenty years you have clothed him in a new livery and a bright shining hat and given him an impressive posture, and a commanding voice. Yet underneath he has remained the same insatiably hungry and insecure Jack.

The time has arrived at last when the inner Jack needs to slow down the coach and bring the horses to a steady quiet pace, while you listen for the voice of the soul maker. Make no mistake about it, the Master within is waiting. He waits for you to affirm and rejoice in the true Jack.

All your life you have run away from inward truth. Everyone does. It is a tendency you have in spades. Your way of denying the realities of your character was to create a false one that your ego could admire. Sometimes I wonder if you really didn't know what was fantasy and what was fact. The strange thing, which I want you to explain to me sometime, is how you could adroitly and unerringly ascertain the facts of your clients' problems and represent them with intuitive brilliance; yet when it came to your own life, you were always in some never-never land. You were about to write some important book on estates and trusts that would have been a definitive text for the law schools. No one ever saw a first draft, nor did you think you might need some help with the research. You had to find ways to demonstrate your success in your career. It had to show—in houses and in a vast array of possessions. You seldom talk about your children because they haven't fulfilled your fantasies for their lives. After Hilary became critically sick, your family began to visit her regularly. It was then that Hilary learned the real facts of your childhood rebellions, your misrepresentations of your family's many years of poverty and anxiety, as well as the full story of your first marriage.

I remember your face that evening in your den. Hilary's feet were propped up on a footrest. We three were sitting together. She began to unroll the scroll of your life story for my benefit, but I know now that she did it mainly for your benefit. It was only as she laughed in that giggly way she had that I realized there was not an ounce of anger in her voice. None of your coils of deception were deception to her. Your expression was one of embarrassed love. You were facing a facet of yourself in the presence of two people who loved you. I wonder if it wasn't the first time you had ever done so. The impressive fact to me was how you sat there quietly listening to it all. I think back on that evening as a time of new birth for you. It was as though Hilary were engaged in the ancient ritual of the Chinese, giving you your very own name for the first time. Love, nonjudgmental, understanding love, presented you with a sacred rose of acceptance—complete acceptance, not of the Jack you would like to be, but of the Jack you are. It was as though the Holy Spirit had broken through and said, "This is my beloved son in whom I am well pleased."

Yes, Jack, I believe without reservation that a new creature is being formed in your depths these days. It was no surprise to me that a few weeks after that occasion in your den, with Hilary as the midwife, you raised with me the history of your fantasies and your problem with veracity. Jack, it isn't a lie that erodes the inner life of a person, however serious the falsehood may be. Even deeper is when we lose sight of the truth altogether. It is one thing to lie; it is another thing to lose a fundamental accountability to the truth within us. A lie can be faced and overcome. Its consequences cannot be recovered. What's done is done. But the damage to the depths can be repaired if we flee from falsehood to the safe haven of a sacred reverence for truth.

I bring this aspect of yourself into focus because it is connected with your original question about self-centeredness. Your sense of the ''I'' of Jack is weak and distorted. You lacked the nourishment of regard and affection that your ''I'' needed. We see the ''I'' of ourselves in the mirrors of other people's eyes. So much of that was tragically neglected in your early life. One way you found to defend yourself from that absence was to fantasize, to misrepresent, to lie when it suited your insatiable hunger for recognition. The coachman changed his hats according to the needs of the moment. Sometimes he struck one pose, sometimes another. It all depended on the passing scene.

Yet, underneath the changing costumes you knew you were Jack Wardman. The real ''I'' of Jack was not altogether lost. Hilary always knew that. I thank God for Hilary's unconditional love of you. The ''I'' of the coachman doesn't need to change his outer apparel any more. He can simply rest in being Jack Wardman and listen for the master within. The horses of conquest and power are worn out. They need a rest, too.

What is the master saying? He is saying, "Let's drive home, and rest with one another a while."

With my love,

J.

Dear Grant,

Thank God for modern medicine. It was a scary time when your blood pressure alerted us to the possibility of a severe coronary episode. We all thought the kidney operation had gone wonderfully. No complications were indicated. We were grateful that people can function quite well on one kidney, and we thought it was only a question of recuperation. Then all sorts of postoperative signals began to flash red lights, and we were in panic about what was happening, although we tried to hide our anxieties from you. This new drug to prevent cardiac arrest was a miracle for us. None of us had heard of it until Dr. Levy explained it to us.

Well now, old friend, the worst is over, and with rest and diet and medication, as well as cooperation and trust, you will be ready to resume a normal life again when winter is over. As I reflect on it all since I came home from our visit, I wonder what I should say.

Serious sickness is an unparalleled opportunity for us if we can only cut through the treatment processes. The incredibly complex and rapid development of modern medicine can be nothing but a cause for thanksgiving, although sometimes we may wonder about it. The consequences of the past and future advances in medical science are only now being carefully studied. Only recently have we realized that the vast increase of options in medical care raises ethical issues of extraordinary complexity.

In the meantime, we who are patients have to fight for our humanity against the enormous increase of medical technology. At its present stage of development the thing is out of balance—the patient can so easily get lost in the appalling scope of treatment. We become pieces of matter, so many feet long, so many pounds heavy, with varying statistics of vital signs attached to our charts, and volumes of notations about our condition. It is not uncommon for medical personnel to fail to look at the patient, face to face, human being to human being. The patient is dehumanized, reduced to the level of an infant who is expected to do what is asked without question or explanation. If the patient insists upon consultations and serious discussion of treatment options, the consequences are often counter-productive because the patient soon learns that a price of alienation has to be paid for what is interpreted as uncooperativeness. Not infrequently, an atmosphere of enmity complicates the treatment procedures when the patient becomes obstreperous or unusually demanding.

To be sure, much of this problem of dehumanizing the patient in medical care is due to the excessive pressures on the medical personnel. They all seem to have too much to do and too little time in which to do it. They haven't the time or the training to be able to sit quietly with the patient and deal with a host of questions and fears, but increasingly

I am convinced such a person is urgently needed in the
treatment process. It should be a knowledgeable, skilled,
and mature person, not someone whose orientation is
primarily psychiatric or medical, but a human being who
deserves to win the confidence of both the medical
caretakers and the patient. Someone needs to be a bridge.
How many times did I have to serve in that capacity
between you and the medical staff in the past two weeks? It
doesn't matter. I'm only glad that the hospital trusted me
and that we trusted one another. As I sit here in my study
thinking back on it all, Grant, these questions of modern
medical care fairly shout aloud to me for attention.

But, of course, it is of other things that I want to write.
I wish the hospital weren't such a frantically busy, noisy,
and crowded institution. There is so little opportunity to
recollect, to enter a quiet place near to the heart of God, to
open ourselves to the Healer with his blessings, not only for
our bodies but for our total being. How often do we have a
legitimate reason to insist on privacy and time to reorder
our lives? What more perfect opportunity is there for us to
set priorities on our values and make some important
changes in our style of life than when we are recovering
from a serious illness? Can you imagine a better time in
which to claim the nearness of the Holy Spirit than in those
hours after the nurses have prepared us for the night and
before sleep kisses our brow? Does Scripture and the
richness of the church's heritage of prayer ever come alive
with as much warmth and glow as during those days of
patient recuperation from a near-death experience?

What an aching loss it is if we don't avail ourselves of
the soul's opportunities during illness, or if the hospital

environment precludes time for such growth! However, Grant, I well realize that in the early stages of your coronary crisis the issue that was uppermost in your mind was not the destiny of your soul, but the future security of your family. How could it be otherwise?

For so long, you were out of a job. The company had just begun to rehire people a month before your hospitalization. Your debts exceed your resources. The kids are still young. Rachel's skills are limited. The job market has almost no place for her. You were desperate with worry about what would happen to the family if you died.

Two people really saved the day for us. One was that wonderful woman from the social services department of the hospital. What a caring and competent person she is! You and Rachel and I sat there like thirsty laborers in the desert as she wrote it all out on a yellow pad for us. Instead of downgrading your fears, she met them head on with facts. She explained, with four children all under fifteen what Rachel's Social Security benefits would be if you were to die. A job-training program for Rachel could be made available as soon as she felt she could leave the youngest long enough to obtain it. Your hospitalization was still in effect, thanks to the union and the company policy. Medicaid was a last resource for the family if you weren't here to provide such care in emergencies. Part-time work could be found for Rachel, to help with the immediate problems if that were necessary. On and on she went! God couldn't have sent us a more wonderful angel than that woman that day.

The second person I'll always be grateful for was your pastor. He not only befriended you and prayed for you and stood by Rachel with faithful support, but he also came up with solid assurance of help. As he explained to you his church's program of lay pastoral care, I marveled at such a church. It was just like New Testament times. He cited examples of families you knew personally. He explained how the church had found housing, clothing, housekeeper assistance, child guidance and care services, food supplements, and financial resources to sustain a desperately needy family in the parish. "We use all the help we can get," he said, "then we supply the rest ourselves."

I asked him about the program later and he said, "You see, we're not a big church. We know each other. We all tithe because we believe we're supposed to help our brothers and sisters when they're in need. We have twelve shepherds in charge of the program. We're extra careful about our money because it's God's money. We haven't let one of our families down yet! Don't worry, we'll be there when Grant and Rachel and the kids need us."

After the full impact of the support from those two great persons seeped through our consciousness, I could see an unmistakable difference in your condition as well as in your questions to me. We've known each other so long, Grant, there are no secrets between us. You call me your confessor, but, Grant, I must say you are a confessor for me also. There is so much about prayer for healing and trust in the love of God that you and I have shared, I thought you might be interested in how all that became real for me when I recently underwent surgery. Although our physical problems were different, many of our responses of the spirit were similar.

A few months ago it became necessary to remove a stone, the size of a small jagged marble, from my bladder, and because of the enlargement of my prostate gland, that had to be removed also. I had a couple of scratchy patches postoperatively, which scared my darling Peggy, but all is well again now as I write. The pathology reports were all reassuring. The old ticker is fully recovered, and life is full of ministry once more.

After surgery my body was aquiver with protest. It had been violated. It raised its voice in unmitigated rage. I lay on a stretcher waiting to be wheeled from the recovery room to my bed. Two nurses stood at either end of the stretcher, waiting for clearance to take me back to my room. Naturally, this was mere routine to them. They exchanged tidbits of gossip with one another. I couldn't stop shaking. I asked for more blankets. I was patted. "Never mind, dearie, we'll soon have you back in your own bed again."

Faceless people in crowded corridors passed me by. Finally, I was shifted from the stretcher to my bed. An irrigation tube and a catheter were attached to me. Antibiotics and glucose were dripping fluid into a vein in my wrist. My blood pressure and heart were being monitored. Samples of urine and blood were being taken to the laboratory for the vital information they would give us. I was given morphine for pain relief, and soon I was asleep.

It was a drugged and frightening sleep. I was disoriented. The bed rail in my hand became a vicious and threatening crowbar. I didn't dare to let go of it for fear of what it might do to me. I tried to pray but it was useless to me. There was no energy available for the effort. Then, unexpectedly, a movie screen appeared on the wall of my imagination. My favorite psalms were printed on it. All I had to do was to read the lines as slowly and silently as I wanted. Psalms 1, 23, 30, 46, 91, 121. Soon I was enfolded in peace. Peggy was standing nearby, perplexed, taut, frightened, not knowing what I was experiencing. I smiled at her dear face and fell to sleep, hands folded on my chest.

On the second night after surgery I awoke around one in the morning with bleeding and severe spasms of pain. It wasn't the first time that stabbing sensation had taken me in its power and elevated my temperature. Morphine had only dulled the problem, and it took some time to be effective. I sat up and involuntarily put my free hand to the location of the pain, as I had done hundreds of times in a healing ministry for others. "Lord Jesus," I whispered urgently, "you've just got to help me out!" Within seconds the pressure and pain I was enduring were relieved, and I sank back on my bed with unspoken gratitude.

I then settled back for sleep. I had not called the nurse. The nightlight cast its faint yellow glow over the room. I looked toward the windows to be sure it wasn't dawn, and there before me was a fluttering white moth hovering above a plant on the window sill, selecting a green leaf on which to settle. Where had the delicate creature come from? Why then? And why there on a plant sent to me by a spiritual son of mine?

I had an experience after my son Peter died in which hummingbirds, butterflies, and night moths became messengers of the eternal kingdom to me. Don't ask me how I knew it, Grant. I just knew they were bringing me messages of assurance and immortality from "beyond." You must recall those days? I never saw, before or since, so many butterflies fluttering and filling the landscape around my house in Rhode Island. Later it was scores of hummingbirds; after sunset it was dozens of night moths clinging to a tree in the forest around me as I shone my flashlight upon them.

I smiled at my precious white-winged night visitor, trembling on a green leaf, waiting to be greeted. "Thank you" was all I said.

Nighttime is a strange mixture in hospitals. It is neither day nor night, but a little of both. There is constant activity. Nurses come and go, checking intravenous feedings, replacing them, regulating their flow, replacing the hundreds of bottles of sodium chloride used to irrigate my bladder to prevent infections or clotting or phlebitis. Sometimes the irrigation tubes would fill with air before a new supply was provided. There was nothing to do but endure the discomfort and wait for the nurse to come. She was always sensitive to my problem and apologetic if the problem was severe. The amount of irrigation had to be monitored, the color recorded, and adjustments made. During the day I scarcely noticed the procedures. They went on for almost two weeks. I became adept at doing the adjustments of the flow myself, but at night, with no book or writing pad to occupy me, I half opened my eyes as the loving steps of the night shift came and went, carrying flashlights, checking my blood pressure, changing the dressings, speaking in low tones.

Sometimes when my door was left ajar, I heard the cries of an elderly soul who had required a hip replacement. She had to be repositioned during the night to avoid bed sores. It was like a knife in me to hear her crying pathetically,

"Mama, Mama, help me." During the day I heard her loud
protests from time to time, but never "Mama." Do you
suppose the elemental call for that primal figure in our lives
belongs uniquely to the night hours, especially if we're in
our eighties?

As you know, Grant, the presence of a person is a
quality I have trained myself to perceive as quickly as the
words we speak to one another. At night the nurses in
change of me spoke few words, but their presences were
inescapable. Some were simply absent. They brought
nothing but skilled hands and medical training. I could
barely make contact with them. Others were solid, good,
faithful persons who communicated a presence of
competence and unchanging compassion. Yet others were
brusque, negative, pressured, irritable, and uncertain. They
had little confidence in themselves. Some were uncommonly
steady, knowledgeable, but with their skills they brought
something else. It was a quality of gentleness and love. I
could sense it from their hands. One particular nurse who
reappeared after her weekend caught my special attention. I
welcomed her back and told her I had missed her. Then I
said, "You pray for your patients, don't you?" She said,
"Yes, I do, but how did you know?" "Osmosis," I
answered.

One night a substitute nurse was on duty. I was lying
on my side, a blessed position I hadn't been able to
accommodate for two weeks. My back was to the door. As
soon as it opened, I shivered with fear. She did everything as
she was supposed to do. I couldn't complain about her
competence, but I couldn't wait for her to leave the room.

What a relief it was to hear the door shut behind her. While she was taking my pressure I dared to look into her eyes. There was a strange malice there. I wonder where she came from and what has happened to her.

Isn't it strange, Grant, how little things can impress us out of all proportion to their reality when we are sick. One afternoon I was admiring the soft orangeish luxuriance of the blossoms on a begonia plant a blessed friend had sent me. One blossom was bent beneath the weight of a green leaf above it. "Let the poor thing lift its head," I said to Peggy.

There must have been some stridency in my voice, for she stood up and nervously tried to see what I saw. We didn't seem able to connect. "This one?" she asked. "No, no. That one there—can't you see under the leaf? No, no, get down at my level and look at the begonia," I said. Then she saw it at once and released the blossom so it popped up between the leafy fulness of the plant. She smiled at me indulgently. The thing had been a major issue with me. She made no comment, except to kiss my forehead. I fell back on my pillows, exhausted. Well, I thought, at least the flower is now free to smile at the sun.

I also remember one lunch when I tried to open a small carton of milk on my lunch tray. My trembling hands couldn't get the stubborn thing open. I gave up and threw it across the room with all the force I could muster. "They glue the damn things with epoxy these days," I said to myself.

And bed pans. Don't you loathe them? From previous experience I had mastered the knack of getting the stupid things under me in time, but I really regard them as evil objects, even though I have settled my hind parts on them with unabashed gratitude and relief.

I do think these experiences of illness are more difficult for those who love us than they are for us. My dear Peggy was wrung dry, squeezed almost beyond endurance. It was our first experience of seeing one of us undergo major surgery, and its consequences, since we were married. She hardly left my side for a week, and I doubt if she slept more than two or three hours a night during that time. I was by that time perfectly sure all would be well, but her unreserved love and dependence on me meant that she went through my illness like a sleepwalker in an unnameable nightmare. When at last she knew all was well, she bounced back to her dear zestful self again. I tried to get her to tell me about her feelings when I was my most miserable, but she couldn't. It isn't her style. All that mattered was that I was ill and she was with me and frozen in her fear. She didn't dare talk about it lest she lost her control and added to my problem. So she counted the hours and then the days and then the weeks. Two months later she could talk about it. That's just the way she is. I love that simplicity and depth in her. Those of us who have to run on at the mouth about everything are in constant danger of becoming superficial and uncentered, and, besides, through the whole hospital experience she didn't have to talk to me about her feelings. It was plain enough on her face and in her nervousness, although each day she wore a different pretty dress to brighten my room.

I must tell you one more striking event of those two and a half weeks, Grant. One night following surgery I awoke with a strange mixture of pain and peace. Spasms of awful discomfort seized me for intervals of a few minutes. The pillow under my head was wet with perspiration. Yet none of these symptoms really troubled my spirit. I felt myself enfolded in a great presence of peace.

I was puzzled by the disparity between my physical discomfort and my spiritual serenity. Was I denying the pain? Was I repressing anxiety about it? The questions were ludicrous. Some important breakthrough of the spirit was imminent. I knew it and I quietly waited to see what was going to happen next. In a moment I was filled with smiles.

A fragrance hovered around my bed. It wasn't the incense of high mass or the fresh aroma of lilies of the valley, but it was a faint mixture of the two. I smiled in silent gratitude. This was exactly a fragrance I had experienced once when I had spent time in the room of Padre Pio, the friar of San Giovanni, whose sanctity I have long venerated and reflected upon. I had also experienced it after a special time of blessing and prayer with Agnes Sanford in a chapel at Whitinsville, Massachusetts. When we clergy asked her about that fragrance, she said, "The prayers of the saints are like incense to the Lord." A great joy came to me in my hospital room that night, for a poor creature of many fractures of the soul like myself had been blessed by the peace of the saints. I personally think it was Padre Pio, but the identity doesn't matter.

Finally, Grant, I have to tell you that the single most sustaining and nourishing characteristic of my experience was the frequent reception of the Eucharist. Both my rector and the curate of our church brought me the spiritual food of the body and blood of our Saviour, every day that first week. I took it into myself as a wondrous strengthening of the Christ within me. "Therefore with angels and archangels and all the company of heaven [I did] laud and magnify his holy name."

Naturally, Grant, I have been asking myself some serious questions because of this experience. One result of the dialogue with myself is that I have at last really absorbed with my emotional self the fact of my age. Until something like this happens I think you put off the reality of old age. In your mind you go on thinking you're fifty or forty-five or even forty, instead of sixty-eight. That's pretty silly, but I think we do it.

The recognition of my stage in the journey made me realize that I needed to ask myself how ready I am to enter the kingdom of everlasting light. To my surprise, I suddenly knew that I am more ready today for that adventure in the Lord than I have ever been in my life. None of us are ever wholly ready, are we? But I would not go kicking and screaming now if I were called to do so. That was a revelation to me.

Another development while in the hospital was my firm resolution not to pressure and crowd myself so heavily from one commitment to another. I am at an age where I have to allow space between commitments, space in which to breathe, to rest, to sail or swim, to walk with my dog, to read a Dick Francis novel, to memorize another Shakespeare passage, to go to the theatre with Peggy, or take the train to New York to see an art restrospective at the Metropolitan both Peggy and I enjoy. During the past year I had slipped back into my old pattern of overscheduling myself. Not again.

Forgive this intolerable tome, Grant, about my scratchy patch with the ills of the flesh. Certain commonalities of our recent bouts with hospitals made me want to share my ups and downs with you. I'm sorry to be so long-winded, but after all those years of bearing with me that should be no surprise to you.

My love to Rachel,

As ever,

Dear Ted and Lil,

Such suffering is too much for me. I am mute before it. Something has been happening to me at this sunset season of my pilgrimage. It is as though a rheostat of my nervous system has been turned up. Every change in the atmosphere affects me. I have always been hypersensitive to the pain of those around me. It is never hard for me to cry. But now I can't turn it off.

I beg you to forgive my grossly selfish musings at the beginning of this letter! You two people have never been far from my spiritual awareness since we first met two years ago. Your sufferings are so much greater than my own. It is the height of audacity to mention my increased vulnerability. I do so only because your recent news has brought the anguish back to me with transporting power.

I shall never forget the time we met. I was speaking at a mission for prayer and healing in California. A friend of yours, whose wife was in the choir, persuaded you to try it. Do you remember your comment to him was "Tim, if he's a yeller I'm going to walk out!" Well, Lil, I've been known to be "a yeller," but thank God that wasn't one of the times.

However, Ted and Lil, *you* have something to holler about! I have had to give one child to the eternal. I can't imagine what it would be like if I had been compelled to give up three! And one at a time, with the same mysterious disease.

Your pain must cry to heaven. I cannot imagine, even in my present state of vulnerability, what it is like to lose one, two, three healthy, happy children, each at the age of one, struck down by an undiagnosed illness, each child dying within weeks of his first birthday, afflicted by a strange immunological deficiency no medical test can describe.

Nor, Lil, can I fathom the courage by which you are now pregnant with a fourth child. No baby was more enveloped by prayer than your Timothy, your last child. Your photos of him at his first birthday must surely have reflected everyone's confidence that God had answered your prayers abundantly. I can see him happy chortling, sitting in his high chair. Even now it is incredible to me to realize that only a few weeks later he was dead. Your whole circle of friends had claimed health for that child, and so had you and Ted. Everyone thought you had made it.

When we talked, only two months after Timothy died, the grief you both felt was devastating. Your faith was at your feet in tatters. I'm afraid I was of little help in trying to get you to believe you could go on believing; but now the marvelous cycle of life goes on again and a new child is on the way! I pray it is a girl—only because the comparisons to the past may be alleviated by a sex difference, and secretly I urgently hope that a female may have a defense against the mysterious killer a male progeny may lack.

There is a vast quantity of human woe that is

unnecessary. With the advances in medical knowledge, and the vast strides in communication and transportation in today's world, it is no exaggeration to guess that ninety percent of major illnesses can be treated satisfactorily. Death cannot be defeated, but it can be delayed. It does seem this is one sorrow that belongs to the category of the defensible. May it be so, dear Ted and Lil, may it be so! Like you, I feel that if we get beyond that first year and the second, we can relax and cry "Home free!"

Ted, you are a doctor of theology after long and arduous graduate study. Why don't you write a commentary on the book of Job? Put your anguish into it, your doubts, your anger, your disdain for any pietistic blatherings that well-meaning friends may have directed at you and Lil. Rage against God. Don't take silence for an answer. Maybe the only answer you will get is the one Job got. Ah, but for you and me that would be surpassing sublime, wouldn't it?

I have only one credit to my name in my relation to God: I have always had the sense to know in my gut that as the heavens are higher than the earth, so are God's ways above my ways and his thoughts above my thoughts. It would be arrogance for me to think God might answer my cries of why, even though desperation has forced the cry from my lips often enough. However, I have repeatedly stormed the heavenly gates to know one solid assurance and it is that the God of our Lord Jesus Christ *is*! If I am given that rock to stand on, I can bear anything.

Ted, claim that encounter. Like Job, you will not get the answers you want, but you will find that God is real. That's all we need, isn't it? His answers will not fit our orthodoxies, but I have learned he does faithfully reveal himself to be real to us—if we find the solitude and the patience to persist in asking him to step across the threshold of our consciousness.

I yearn for you and Lil to have that epiphany. Knowing you, it might well become the mystic certainty of a divine presence irradiating your astonished consciousness. My experience has left me with an unnameable peace. Questions are irrelevant. Divine explanations are an offense. I would not dare to pose them. All I know is that I am, and God is, and out of his holy sovereignty his mercy has bent down to touch me with his terrible joy.

The first time it happened to me was as a child of seven. I was transfixed by a morning glory, clustered in crowded company on a wall I passed on my way to second grade. I looked into the face of one, and God smiled back at me! Nor was it radically different when God spoke a word of comfort to me three hours after the news of the sudden death of my son by an automobile accident. It has ever been thus with me. A breakthrough comes. It brings no content of theological proportions. I have but a fragmentary notion of that incomparable experience of Moses. "Whom shall I say you are?" he asks God, eager for more, like all of us, more ever more. The only answer he gets is "I am who I am," or as it could be translated, "I am the one who is."

Now, my dears, I cannot deny that I want so much more for you both as I join your many friends in praying for the birth of this new child. I want the child to be enormously blessed with vitality, able to ward off any infection, growing stronger every day, celebrating a first, second birthday with preteens to follow and all that comes after that! But no matter how it turns out, more than

anything else I want you to sense the undeniably real
presence of Christly love around you every step of the way.

The grief you have experienced in unbelievable
repetition has driven me again to define for myself where
the rock can be on which to stand before such tragic
innocent suffering. After my first wife died, and after Peter
died, I wrote a little book in which I tried to do that, but
time has passed since then and the ship of my journey has
accumulated more barnacles, and I have sailed over new
seas.

The Korean flight 007 was one of them. A shining
eager-faced loving girl I had known since a child went down
in that flight. She and her husband were on their way to
Japan. Her smile, radiant with new knowledge of the quest
of the spirit she had pursued in India, is as vivid before me
now as though we had talked but an hour ago. A year ago
at her school we planted a Japanese red maple tree at the side
of a rock that bears a plaque recording her name and her
death.

Not long ago I visited the black wall in Washington. It
is highly polished granite bearing the names of 58,000
persons who died in the Vietnam War. The names are
carved in the stone in the order in which they died. The
names have a rhythm about them: C. Washington Jones,
Ulysses A. Johnson, Merrill P. Hanson. People come at all
hours of the day and the night to find a name. They trace it
with trembling fingers. They try to perch a small flower
somewhere nearby. Sometimes they leave a favorite toy
behind. You can see their faces mirrored in the stone,
shining tears reflected on the polished surface.

Two lovers were walking slowly behind me. The young

woman said to her friend in disbelief, "Just think! All those people are dead," to which he replied, "Jesus Christ, let's not let it happen again." He didn't know he was speaking the prayer of my heart as I walked heavily away from the black wall.

I know from my own experience in World War II that one of the most horrible traumas to overcome was not the near miss to your own life in combat service; it was the hot guilt you felt because you came out untouched and your buddy, only a few feet from you, was mutilated beyond recognition, with his body splattered over a radius of a hundred yards.

My own father's death, due to a freak accident at a railroad crossing, left my mother a demolished woman with seven children to raise. She pulled herself together within a couple of years and achieved her task beyond the wildest expectations of those who knew what she had before her, but it was a tragic, irreplaceable loss to her and to seven growing children.

The litany of tragic experience has no end. Knock on any door and each home has its story to tell. There are no glib answers, as there are no glib stories. I wish people would have the common courtesy to hug the sorrowing and walk away, with wet cheeks, only to return with unobtrusive gestures of quiet practical help, again and again. Words don't belong, sometimes. Silence is better.

However, I have often been helped by the printed word, and maybe you will find a crumb of comfort in something I have written; so I shall try to put down my most recent insight for you, ridiculously inadequate though it is. It all revolves around the most ludicrous idea of divine humility.

You know in your New Testament studies, Ted, how occasionally you come on a seminal insight in your biblical work, and suddenly the whole thing is brimming over with it. That has been happening to me ever since I became acquainted with Padre Pio of San Giovanni, the Capuchin friar who, like St. Francis, bore upon his body the five wounds of the crucified Christ, called the stigmata.

I have visited the friary in which he lived for fifty years until his death. I have spent time in the friary of the town in southern Italy where he was born and raised. I have spent hours in prayer on the hills and in the fields where he labored as a boy. I have harvested grapes and figs from the ground where he lived. I have sat long hours in the barren small rooms in which he was born, protected from the Adriatic storms of winter and spring. I have talked with people who knew him. I have seen a film in which he celebrated the Holy Mass. I have sat staring for long hours at the confessional in which he listened to the guilt and sin of thousands who made long pilgrimages to southern Italy to receive the purification and absolution that only Padre Pio could give with unique authority. I have sat a long night in the corner of his room, separated by an iron grille, studying each detail of that place where this sainted man prayed and wept and slept.

I have been stupefied by the bloodied linen bandages he wrapped about his body to dress the wound on his side. I have blinked almost uncomprehendingly at the scales of blood a loving friar had scraped from his hands and his feet before applying a new dressing. I have been puzzled how he had managed to collect them and preserve them, because Padre Pio was firm in his instructions that as little attention as possible should be brought to his stigmata—duplicates of the flower of Assisi and above all of the suffering servant of God dying on his cross at Golgatha.

For fifty years, from the time it began on September 23, 1918, until fifty years later when he died on September 19, 1965, Padre Pio suffered excruciating pain from these wounds. Many physicians examined him. Many prescribed treatment, meticulously monitored. Over the years no one in the medical community could diagnose the phenomenon adequately. Lesions were described to the millimeter. Blood flow was measured. Nothing changed. The wounds defied diagnosis. They refused to respond to treatment and they never became infected.

When Padre Pio elevated the host at the crucial time in the Mass, new blood dripped from his hands. Priests assisting him were prepared to bandage his wrists. His rapt gaze at the chalice, held for long periods, while weeping caused many in the congregation frequently to exclaim, "He sees the Christ." Those who were there tell me they will never forget it. In that celebration of the Eucharist he was the suffering Christ, suffering for the sins of the world today. No one who ever saw it doubted the truth of what was happening at that altar; nor do I.

Padre Pio has become a part of me. He guides me. He rebukes me. He forgives me. He leads me. He holds me in a powerful grip. I am no longer free to follow my own will. When I try to ignore him, Elijah-like, he stands in my way. By now it's become a joke between us. He laughs gently at my silly evasions.

More than anything else, however, there is the abysmal anguish that Padre Pio communicates to me. His identification with the personal and historical tragedies of our time is beyond description. It is a moan of heaven that fills the universe. I hear only the faintest echo of it. Anything more would exceed human endurance. Pio is the Christ-man sent to suffer for the modern world. He is another sign of God's humble love for his creation, sharing our suffering in an intensity no human could possibly fathom, yearning to save us from ourselves.

It seems to me, Ted, that the whole history of the Bible is the story of God reaching out in loving humility to embrace his creation and his creatures. He does so with consummate patience and suffering love. Moses repsonds and his people rebel. Their enemies are too strong. There is nothing to eat. Water is nowhere to be found. Faith fails. The urge to go back to safety, even if it be slavery, is overpowering. The gods of other tribes are more promising. Their tribal demands are less overpowering. They have no judges to rebuke them. Their prophets are the lackeys of the king. They have no Nathan to point a judging and accusing finger at the king and wither him to penitence as he says, "Thou art the man." There is no Jeremiah or Isaiah to woo and warn them to return unto the Lord "while he may be found."

What a unique, unrepeatable love story it is—the Lord of patience seeking his own again and again, only to be rejected again and again. Finally the eyes of Isaiah gleam with anticipation. The Messiah's time is drawing near. The Eternal sends his only begotten son, but the story is the same. Suffering, patient, humble love tries again only to be rejected again.

And with what humility the deed is done. A babe is

wrapped in swaddling clothes. A maid has consented to give the external human flesh. The child is born in a stable. God's humility becomes a defenseless newborn infant. The Almighty is helpless. And how does it end?

They taunt the child of Bethlehem, now become a man. He is nailed, hands and feet, to a cross. A sword pierces his side. "If you are the Son of God, come down from your cross now," they cry. Three hours later he hangs his head and dies. "It is finished," he murmurs. His end is as humble as his beginning, and both are surrounded with suffering. In pain his mother brought him forth, and in pain his heavenly Father brought him to his kingdom. As the heavenly being has suffered the rejection of his people, so now the only begotten son has suffered the hatred of his own. Father and Son are locked together in a common bond of sorrowful love for a world that tragically blocks the purifying flow of Christ consciousness.

Ted and Lil, it is the story of the human race. Since the beginning of time it has even been thus between God and his world. My point in laboring the issue is ever so personal. If the Bible is a revelation of our relation to the God of the universe, then his suffering humble love must apply to our personal tragedies of innocent suffering and pain. His suffering shares our suffering. His rejection must identify with our experience of rejection. His sorrow must permeate our sorrow.

At the nadir point of divine sorrow, two unforgettable cries have rung down the ages. One was "Father forgive them for they know not what they do." Many years ago, Bernanos implored us on bended knee and with hollowed sorrowful eyes to forgive God. He said, "God gave us the

intolerable burden of freedom. In such a world there will be
tragedies and sorrow and loss and pain and tears. It cannot
be otherwise, unless you want to eradicate your humanity.
To be human, made in the image of God, is to be free to
suffer and to inflict suffering. Live with this inescapable
weight. It is both your burden and your glory.''

But, my dears, I would rather live in a world of growth
and change, of freedom and choices, responsible for my own
soul, than in a world of unblemished happiness from which
all possibilities of tragedy were banished from the human
scene. When we withdraw from God in angry
unforgiveness, wishing that creation were ordered
differently, we "know not what we ask." When we meet
the anguish of life with complaining anger against God,
there is a secret beneath our complaint. We privately think
we are exempt from the grief and suffering of most people.
We wish the world were made differently so that disease
and accidents, violence and creulty, tragedy and senseless
death, poverty and injustice were not options for us in the
human story. In short, Ted and Lil, we rebel against the
way God has made us.

The other cry from that darkness was "My God my
God why hast thou forsaken me?"

Ted and Lil, no other word of Scripture is as dear to me
as that cry from the God-man. The times are without
number when I have hugged it to my breast as the breath of
life itself. I could surrender other sentences of the gospel,
but never that one. In my times of deepest distress it is that
cry I cling to. That sentence tells me as nothing else does
that when I am faced with a wound that can never heal I
have a companion of sorrow to share it with me. When I

came away from our visit after your Timothy's death and his bright jam-smeared face on his first birthday came back to me, I could only repeat, "My God, my God, why hast thou forsaken me?"

Ted and Lil, we're not alone when we walk the slippery paths of hell. Hold fast to him. His suffering patient love will never let us go. Now we see through a glass darkly, one day it will not be so.

Meanwhile, my heart is yours. That baby soon to be born in autumn is going to be perfection itself. I'll be there on the first birthday to kiss you all!

Peace and trust, my darlings,

Joe +

My dear Philip,

I remember a conversation we had years ago when you let me in on your secret. You asked me, "Does a man have the right to take his own life?" I was wholly unsuspecting. *You exuded health and prosperity.* Your leadership is widely recognized. You have innate grace and style. Your company has increased its sales and prestige because you have an amazing capacity to find the people with exactly the right talent to produce what the public will buy. You have commanded the respect and affection of everyone who works for you. Even those you have felt compelled to fire, speak well of you.

Yet you sat quietly in your New York apartment that day, asking me something you've never mentioned before, "Does a man have the right to take his own life?"

Forgive me if I failed to pick up immediately on the anguish that lay behind the question. I leapt to the only conclusion the evidence would seem to have dictated. I asked, "Are you suffering from a terminal disease, Philip?"

It was when you looked straight at me and said, "Doesn't everyone suffer from a terminal disease?" that I knew we were dealing with a problem deeper than physical illness. I felt I was staring into a bottomless black hole. I should have known something was wrong when you took a year's leave of absence from the company.

In the conversation that followed, everything stood before us, unadorned, unprotected, starkly real. I remember it all. You said, "I am no longer the master of my life. Feelings in me come and go like the whimsy of the wind. Every task is a mountain I can never climb. When I try to think, I am unable to put one thought next to another. It all becomes a jumbled confusion. I have given up trying to understand myself. Now and then the weather clears and I say, 'Today will be different. I shall call someone and we'll meet for coffee.' Then suddenly it's all too much of an effort. I reach for the telephone, and my hand drops at my side. 'What's the use,' I say to myself.

"When I'm in the apartment, I turn on the tube. It's my only friend. I fall asleep during most of the stuff, except for the news. I don't know why the news is a compulsion for me, but it is. I watch different channels and commentators for hours. The sight of starving babies in Africa makes me bawl like a child. A pathetic mother holding her infant to a breast that has no milk leaves me a weeping mess. A report of bag ladies and drunks being picked up by the police and taken to the armory where they can sleep and be protected from the cold of winter fills me with infinite sadness. A kid breaks into an old woman's apartment. He rapes her and steals six damn bloody dollars, and I stand up and scream at the top of my lungs at the police. Why don't they catch the bastard and put him in jail? I listen to all the doubletalk about getting rid of the

goddamned nuclear bombs, everybody being so f———
wordy, and I start breaking the dishes in my kitchen.

"Then in the middle of the night I wake up and the
whole world seems hopeless to me. I lie on my bed crying
helplessly because I know nothing is going to improve.
We'll blow ourselves up one day. Stupid as I am, even I can
see that.

"People kill people every day. It happens in my city a
dozen times every night, and New York is not that different
from all the cities in the land. It happens to people in Iran
and Iraq as though human beings were insects. It happens in
Nicaragua and El Salvador because great big strong brother
America to the north is so goddamned afraid of the
Commies he doesn't know how to lick them at their own
game, except with bullets and bombs. Kill, kill, kill. On
and on it goes until the whole damn planet will be finished.
In my rage, all I can do is cry and scream until I am
exhausted and fall asleep. Sometimes I see the sun come up,
trying to shine through my filthy windows."

Philip, I often think that people like yourself are the
most sensible persons on earth. Your nervous system is like
a powerful magnetic field that draws all the sharp steely
filings of the atmosphere unto itself. It is a field of tragic
pain that is hypersensitive to the ubiquitous tragedies of
violence, stupidity, cruelty, and loneliness. It is a burden of
your nature, but it equips you to be a voice of truth that
ought to be heard around the world. Most of us come into
this life with a protective covering around the threads of our
nerves. People like you seem to be born with no protective
covering. You are excruciatingly vulnerable. Every pain you
encounter is magnified by thousands of decibels. What most

of us hear as an underground thud, you hear as a blast of enormous dynamite.

Psychoanalysis has something to tell us about your extreme sensitivity. Lithium and tranquilizers help. They all muffle the horrendous screams of tragedy. Normal life becomes bearable, and you can carry on your responsibilities. I cannot fail to be grateful for anything that lessens your pain. Yet I must tell you that your extremities of agony have taught me much I would not have felt otherwise. Our world desperately needs your kind of person.

Your reactions to love and beauty come to my mind. Not long ago at the vernal equinox, and at a time when a full moon almost coincided with it, we had a tumultuous storm roar out of the northeast. You and I stood on my porch in Rhode Island. The sound of the surf on the other side of the marsh pond was deafening. You put your hands to your mouth and shouted, "Let's go over to the beach and see it." I agreed but cautioned you to put on boots and cap and woolen scarf. I knew it would be bitterly cold.

When we arrived a few minutes later, the sun was beginning to sink behind us to the west. Far out on the horizon the rays of the sun picked up millions of fluttering colorful fish scales quivering on the surface of the sea. The crashing ominous sound of the surf made conversation impossible. It was all I could do to stand up against the wind. We advanced perhaps one hundred feet. Your tall figure was beside me. I clutched your young arm for support. I said, "Philip, I think we'd better go back." "No, no," you cried, "God, it's so beautiful! I've never seen anything so beautiful!" Before I knew what had happened, you let go of me and ran directly into the wind, rushing down to the line where the surf was protesting wildly against the shore. Then you stopped dead still. In a second, the water was almost to your waist. You stretched out your arms and embraced the elements. I shouted, "Philip, Philip, come back, come back." Of course, you couldn't hear me. I felt sick. My stomach emptied its contents on the sand. When I stood up again, you were walking toward me, smiling, laughing, roaring your joy in it all. "Have you ever seen anything so beautiful in your life?" you asked me. When we got home you were still flying high in your praise of the experience.

Subsequently, I asked if you had realized what danger you were in as you waded into the ocean. "Why? How so?" you queried. "Another five feet and the surf would have destroyed you through the power of the undertow," I answered. "Oh, my God!" was all you said.

I suppose it is your imperviousness to danger that excites and fascinates the women who are drawn into your special circle, or could it be that they instinctively connect to that need of yours to push yourself to the brink of the abyss! Do they see themselves as your protectors, destined to save you? Certainly it is not your big hulking frame that draws them to you with such ease. You are abundantly gifted with a quiet, shy charm that is expressed mainly in that low halting voice of yours. But I don't think animal magnetism or protectiveness or charm explain your love life. They are merely outward symptoms that play conveniently into your hands.

Why is it that in spite of the absences when your depressions render you nonfunctional, there is always a woman available to you for support and comfort? It has never been the same one. The more you tell me about your life, the more convinced I am that you are a man who is compelled to have many relations with many women, at different places and at the same time.

Surely it is not a coincidence that when one of your romantic relationships approaches the real possibility of marriage, you experience a tailspin into the snake pit of depression. Occasionally, you have had to be hospitalized. When you come out of the hospital, the intimacy is broken.

Do not think, Philip, that I see this pattern as conscious or deliberate. I don't think you can help yourself. Some unconscious conflict and anxiety are triggered by an intimacy that claims a complete commitment from you. Philip, you know that your need to love and to be loved is prodigious. Given your passionate extremities, it is not surprising that no one woman can fulfill the monstrous hunger you have for love. Yet you are paralyzed in these relationships. You are as vulnerable as a young deer hovering at the edge of highway 95. You yearn to love intensely, and at the same time you are petrified of the real thing. I wonder why? One clear insight comes to me. It is but one facet of a complex problem.

You and I have often talked about the overshadowing power of your father. There was an almost symbiotic bond between the two of you. He thought your brilliance and acumen in the business world far outshone anything he could ever do, and you thought his strength and imagination far outdistanced any ability you possessed. You fought for his love and you fought against it. Each of you admired the other, but neither of you understood the other.

He made you a friend, a companion, a colleague, while you knew you were still a child, or at least a boy. I wonder if that was the beginning of what you so often call your "mask of deceit." You have told me many times that to the world you are a big, lovable oaf, but to yourself you are a fraud.

I suspect you have never loved anyone so much as you have loved your father. More than once you have said to me, "He made me unhappy out of love." To love someone who brings us suffering is to love in truth and in deed. But why, Philip, did your father's love bring you suffering? Was it because you could not bear to hurt him, when every nerve in you cried out to strike back at your dependence on him? Remember, he, too, suffered the depths of depression but not as violently or as openly as you have known them. Yet, in so far as I know, you never acknowledged those turbulent moods to one another.

Wasn't it strange that when you were hospitalized briefly at Payne Whitney he could never bring himself to visit you? No matter where he was, however, he always left word for me to get through to him after my visits with you. Nor did I ever question why it was you never complained about his absences. Then I realized neither of you could bear the pain a visit would cost the other. It was love that kept you apart. You loved him, although his manipulations and misjudgments brought conflict and unhappiness into your life. Did you always know that whatever he did, he did it out of love for you?

And now your father has been dead for more than a year. It's ironic how a death can catapult someone into a new chapter of wholeness and hope in life. It all depends upon where you are in your journey and at what stage you were in when the beloved one died. You said to me, "I no longer hear the chains rattle when I walk."

This brings me to the essence of this long letter, Philip. You asked me, "Does a man have the right to take his own life?" The answer, of course, is no. To take such responsibility into your own hands is to put yourself in the place of God. "Such wisdom is too high for us. We cannot attain to it."

There is, as you must know by now, a sickness behind such a question. When the instinct to live, to move on, to change, to give and receive, weakens until the taste of life has become unbearable, there is an illness that takes possession of the soul. Everything is open to question. Trust becomes impossible. Friends, even loyal and beloved friends who have stood with us through everything, are turned away. Nothing works. Confusion and weakness hold us down.

Thank God, Philip, someone was always there when that black hole beckoned you with such horrible power into its darkness. It could easily have been otherwise, since it was only afterward that you told us of that moment of fascination with the end as thought and deed were about to become one. You have told me you didn't know what you were doing in that trancelike state. It was as though you were powerless to do anything else, and, Philip, I believe it! It coincides with similar experiences I have heard from others.

But now something new and glorious is beginning to break through. "I no longer hear the chains rattle when I walk," you said. Psychoanalysis could help us understand why the death of your father has brought the promise of freedom from the black hole. I only know that you no longer feel responsible for him or for his depressions, nor do you feel any need to be angry at and guilty toward him for asking more from you than you could give. After your last lucid conversation with him, you told me you felt no conflict when he said, "Remember you have always been the greatest joy of my life." As you went down in the elevator that evening at the hospital, you said you felt the elevator should be going the other way. Something holy was in embryo at that minute.

I must come right out with it, Philip. You are experiencing the birth pangs of the Eternal these days. Yours is a nature that is capable of immense depths. You have a hunger for the infinite. You have sought it in beautiful art, in beautiful music, in beautiful houses and natural scenery. You have sought it in love relationships. Every intimacy in your life began with the hope of the infinite at its center. Yet in all this searching you were acutely conscious that nothing lasts. No love endures. No beauty remains. Everything is transitory. You saw death as the companion of love as well as of beauty. The tenuousness of life has been a constant shadow over your soul.

All this reaching has had an overcast of fevered intensity. It has been both negative and positive; but now the spell has broken, and a time of momentous opportunity is at hand for you. The hour is a crucial one, Philip. You could quietly give thanks for your new freedom and pursue the same bachelor style of life you have pursued for the past twenty-three years, only to find it empty and meaningless twenty-three years from now. Or you could employ the sufferings, the sensitivities, the depths, the yearnings you have known so well in the growth of the soul. If you choose the way of prayer and faith, I can guarantee that persons with your gifts become rare and wonderful persons in the service of Christ's humble love. Your life could be like a tree planted by the river of God.

Should you decide seriously to open yourself to the unique province of religious experience and commit yourself to a steadfast attention to one who seeks to be your Lord, worthy of infinite adoration and obedience, please come to see me. We will need time for much quietude and reflection. There is a holy preparation that should begin, and there are spiritual disciplines that you will have to learn. I pray that it may be so, not only because I know it will be an inexpressible joy to the Lord, but because I know this is your destiny and the path of true happiness for the ongoing pilgrimage of your soul.

Peace and love,

Dear Mary,

I wish I knew the magic words to assuage your grief and to lift the veil a little between this world and the next. Unfortunately, it doesn't work that way. I have asked myself, how can I help Mary to believe in the next world? How can I persuade her that all is well with her Alan in that sphere?

I can tell an unbeliever what I sincerely believe about personal survival of the soul beyond death or see as the meaning of life, the nature of God, or the lordship of Christ, but what I say is weak tea compared to something that comes through me, all unbeknown to myself. Experience is far more powerful than speaking. People remember who you are and what you experienced long after they've forgotten what you said.

Faith is nourished by sanctity, more than by doctrines. The thing is paradoxical. People who are graced by sanctity never talk about it because they don't know they are blessed by it, but it is the most powerful influence for eternity in the world. Holiness is not made for this sick, celebrity-hungry TV world. Its influence springs from the smallest kernel in the earth, like a mustard seed. When it flourishes, there are many souls that take refuge under its branches, but the tree hardly knows what shade it gives because it is preoccupied with the elemental process of growth and giving glory to God.

I have been blessed by a number of holy souls, one of the earliest of whom was my first confessor, Friar Johnson, of the Society of St. John the Evangelist. As a young man in my twenties, I used to make regular retreats at the Cowley Fathers' monastery to which he had come from England many years previously. I was then a poor, mixed-up, frightened, inexperienced Presbyterian minister. Yet from the first moment when I worshipped at that monastery I knew somehow I had found the home of my soul. The person who caught my rapt attention was Friar Johnson.

He could be heard many minutes before his arrival in the chapel because due to his lameness he carried a stout staff, instead of a cane. Clump, clump, he drew nearer from the cloister. Then he would shuffle into his assigned chair and pass from sight as he bent over in prayer, for what seemed to me to be an impossible period of preparation. I used to wonder what this devout and holy man had to say to the Lord that took such an interminable length of time. Of course, he knew all the prayers and offices by heart. At the end, he clumped out the way he had come.

From the first time I saw him, I knew this was the man I needed to take my pathetic misshapen soul in hand. I asked for an appointment with him, and so there began a seventeen-year friendship between Friar Johnson as my confessor and myself as the supplicant. I shall believe to the end of my life that it was Friar Johnson's prayers for me that saved my life through the Second World War and through many crises that followed. His bald head, with its gray fringe, his glasses, which hung perpetually halfway down his nose, his tall hunched thin figure shuffling along the corridors of the monastery, invariably struck involuntary veneration in me. I honored him as one whose presence was holy.

Until I came to know Friar Johnson, my stubborn Presbyterian soul forbade me to pray for the dead. I'm sure my mother thought such a practice belonged to the works of the devil, but Friar Johnson prayed for the dead. At his solemn request, I sent him the names of my dead comrades in my letters to him during the war. How could I refuse him? So I, too, prayed for them. Soon it seemed like the most natural thing in the world. "Why," I asked, "should death terminate loving thoughts and wishes for those we have loved long since and lost awhile?" Love bade me to do it then, and love has kept me at the task ever since.

In the last years of his life, Friar Johnson was too weak to see many people, but he never failed to extend that extraordinary kindness to me. At the end of each visit I came away wondering if I would ever see him in this flesh again. Each time there was an increase of transparency. His body emanated light! I couldn't take my eyes from the phenomenon. His humble confidence in the nearness of his translation from this world to the next was a natural anticipation. He didn't speak of it. The matter required no discussion. His very being was simply radiant with resurrection. Words would have been an affront. We both just knew! The phenomenon was a gift of sanctity. It was not the first time I had observed it, nor was it the last. That man gave me a glimpse of the next world. It wasn't by words that he did it. It simply happened because he was who he was.

The last confession that I made through his ministry was within months of his death. I knew there would not be another. Consequently, I had prepared as carefully and fully as possible for our time together. He sat sideways in a chair with a hand cupped to his right ear, leaning his elbow on the arm rest, concentrating on my every word. I knelt at his side on the bare floor. We were alone in the chapel. I whispered my confusion, beginning, "Father, I have sinned against God and man and I am no more worthy to be called thy son . . . "

It was a crisis time in my spiritual journey. There was much to be confessed, much to be rectified, and much to be forgiven. The root of my vanity and rebellion needed to be torn from the ground of my self-sufficiency.

Friar Johnson's impatience was evident to me from the start. He moved his rough-hewn stick from one side to the other. He shifted positions several times. I didn't know what it meant. His attitude on previous confessions had been almost monumental, not even a foot stirred. Now, it seemed he couldn't contain himself. Halfway through my anguished recital he broke in. "My boy, you needn't go on with that rubbish any longer. All we need to know is do you want God to change your life. Do you desire it without reservation? Will you put his word above you own?"

When I agreed as one only agrees to a spiritual director whose authority you have accepted unconditionally, he pointed to the altar and said, "Go over there and prostrate yourself face down before his holy presence until you are so

uncomfortable you can't stand it any longer. Make your
confession to him. Say all the decades of the rosary as many
times as it takes until you are so exhausted you can barely
get up again." He then made the sign of the cross on my
head and gazed at me with the most loving look I had ever
seen on his drawn face. A few moments later, as I lay on the
chancel's marble floor, I heard his stick clumping step-by-
step into the distance.

I never saw him again except on the night after he died.
I was awakened from a sound sleep. "Friar Johnson," I
cried. His figure was before me. He stood straighter than I
had ever seen him. His strong staff was gone. He looked at
me. There was no smile, only love in his eyes. Then it was
over. I leaned back on my pillows. "He's dead," I said.
Then I knew I had used the wrong word. "He's risen," I
should have said. That's what St. Paul would have said.
Why shouldn't I?

Mary, I could go on and on with stories of personal
encounter of souls I have loved here and known there. The
two worlds are not as separate as we think. By now I have
easily buried well over a thousand people. The number of
times when I was present at their deaths to anoint them and
commit them to God's mercy are in the hundreds. It is
never a perfunctory rite. The mystery of the event invariably
grasps me with a palpable hand. Generally other people are
around me, yet there have been countless times when I was
alone with the patient. Sometimes the impression is
overwhelmingly real, particularly when the dying person
and I are the only ones in the room. It doesn't matter if the
patient is conscious or unconscious. The phenomenon is the

same. A strange process begins at the moment of death. In the lonely silence I sit there gripped by the mystery of it. Something undeniably real happens. The soul is forming its new body, slowly emanating from its previous habitation. There is no difference between the persons emerging in their new bodies and their former manifestation. The person is the same person. The thing that is radically different is the environment into which the person is reborn.

Two more personal experiences illustrate my point. When my first wife died, I sat alone with her body at the undertaker's. It was a selfish need. I had many things I wanted to say to her, and there were many things she had said to me, especially in the last couple of years of our life together, that I wanted to remember and write down in my journal. After a couple of hours had passed and I sat with my pen relaxed in my hand, I knew incontrovertibly that she had simply stood up and walked out of the room. A moment previously she was there. Now she was gone. In a funny way, I was both sorrrowful and reassured. A part of me said, "She's gone!" Another part said, "Praise God, all is well. She couldn't wait any longer." A surpassing peace filled my heart. In the next year she returned, as is always the case with me, awakening me from my sleep.

When my son died, I sat in the same room for the same reasons. His presence was so real, it was unendurably painful. There was no peace available, nor was there any for two or three years. His was a troubled spirit. Repeatedly, he impressed me with his extreme anger. I did not think he was angry with me. There was no doubt about the source of his rage. He died suddenly on a New Hampshire road. The axle of the car broke on a soft shoulder. The car went out of control. In one minute his bright, happy life, full of promise, was before him. Hours later, he was dead.

In the days that followed the funeral, I knew Peter resented his death intensely. Mirrors fell off their hooks. Doors slammed. Family plans were thwarted. His night visits were not mournful; they were images of a very angry young man. I began to speak to him roughly. "Peter, it can't be helped. It was no one's fault. You are only making yourself a prisoner of that limbo where dead souls remain until they accept their destiny. Now stop this unneedful rage! It will get you nowhere, and you are only making our grief more and more intolerable."

We engaged in dialogues of a similar character for some time. Somewhere around the third year, they ceased, and I came to an unshakable certainty that the battle was over. Peter had moved on to another plane of existence—far beyond my reach. I made a retreat that day for the ongoing peace of his soul—from glory to glory.

My experience is not unique. The only aspect of my relation to the people I love who are in the next sphere of being that could be slightly unusual is that I continue to be in touch with them. I don't understand it. The thing has nothing to do with psychic gifts. I don't understand what people mean by a trancelike state in which they communicate with "dead souls." That region of experience is beyond me. I do not wish to denigrate it. The body of evidence is worthy of our serious reflection. I am open to whatever valid insight we might receive from such folks, but it is not my calling. It may belong to some who are better prepared for it than I am, but it is not my cup of tea.

Nevertheless, the presence of many people I love and many people to whom I have been close at the time of their deaths has been so frequent and so real that I am no longer surprised by it. It is not a question of receiving messages for the living or asking questions of the dead. It is the elemental irrefutable encounter between my consciousness and that cherished person's presence. We meet. We are almost palpably real to one another. The scene varies. The circumstances are different. The one constant, however, is the living reality of the other person. We are known to one another.

I have often compared the experience to the dream world, and yet that is only an analogy. It isn't a dream. I am not asleep. I may be meditating or praying or quietly thinking of the dead person, but I am neither slumbrous nor half-conscious, as in the deep silences of meditative techniques.

It has become a certainty with me that anyone can be in touch with loved ones in a similar manner. Generations of primitive man, for thousands of years, possessed the knack of this awareness. For at least five hundred years, we've lost the trick. The capacity has atrophied. For lack of use, we no longer recognize the possibility of its value. I don't understand why it is such a natural function in me except that death was an enormous shadow in my earliest consciousness and as a child I tried assiduously to build a bridge between the two worlds.

Two conclusions from a lifetime of experience in this realm have become inescapable for me, Mary. One is that we all survive the experience of death. Your Alan is alive in the many-mansioned kingdom as surely as St. Francis is.

The one who really knew above and beyond all others told us that if that realm were not real, that if it were but an illusion, some projection of human desire, some form of denial of death's waste and tragedy, he would have told us, for he said, "I am the truth." By its very nature, truth can not contradict itself.

I have a lifetime of experience that adds not one jot or tittle to that assurance, but I can say with all the angels in heaven and on earth: Amen and amen. That world is real, and it is the destiny of all of us to inherit it through the birth pangs of death. I cherish the image he gave us of a many-mansioned kingdom. That suggests to me a habitation of openness and grandeur. It is no narrow realm into which we are squeezed and constrained. It is no single sphere restricted to some happy few. Its proportions are inclusive and boundless.

The second conclusion, Mary, is the sticky one. The best way I know to put it is to say there is no escape from the law of consequences. There are no exceptions. The same law applies inexorably to all of us, no matter what doctrines our minds have embraced or how deeply our hearts have loved. All lives have consequences. The one inescapable reality is character. People can confess all kinds of beliefs, but if those doctrines have left no imprint on the shape of their characters, the consequences of judgment are inevitable. People can have loved many persons and performed many deeds of kindness and generosity, but if the essential person is fixed in narcissistic self-serving motivation, the consequences of judgment in the next realm are fearsome. People can be prodigiously committed in time and energy to the gospel, but if that commitment is a mask that merely conceals an unquenchable drive for power and prestige, the consequences of judgment are horrendous.

Do you see, Mary, why I pray for the dead? Growth, the painful processes of purification, the work of redemption, doesn't stop with death. Hundreds of people have come to my vision after their deaths, and I can only say I have burned with a consuming fire. They needed prayer without cease, far more than my poor little capacities could provide. That's where the communion of saints becomes such a powerful comfort.

In Alan's case, as in the case of my first wife, Carola, it is as though the purification had completed its work here. Each of them was bathed in a luminous light when they came to me, and each moved on quickly to a realm that outdistances the grasp of anyone I know on this side.

I had that same experience recently with a woman named Theresa, in her middle forties, whose friendship I came to possess through the hospice program. She was petite, sandy-haired, round-faced. She chose the hospice program because she needed the help it could provide her and she knew her expected life span was less than six months.

All of us on the hospice team fell in love with her. She was brave as well as realistic. She showed no sign of self-pity, which might have impeded her fervent desire to die in a way that would be an example and a blessing to her family. She was a cooperative patient. She accepted help not only for herself but was even more eager for the social worker to support her family. She made friends with the visiting nurse who called at her home regularly, sometimes in the night, to administer the exact dosage of palliative medication. She wouldn't accept a dosage gracefully that would put her out of consciousness, and naturally she was impatient when the dosage was insufficient to alleviate the need. Our nurses were highly skilled in palliative medicine, and Theresa knew by experience that exact medication was available to make life both conscious and tolerable. She used to say, "There's no excuse for having to bear this much pain, and there's no excuse for knocking me out like a vegetable."

Not long before her death, at our weekly case conference, Theresa's name came up for extended discussion. We were all there—the director of volunteers, the social worker, the nurse in charge of her case, the medical director, and myself as the clergy coordinator.

The nurse said, "Someone needs to help Theresa to open up. She's wonderful! We all know that, but underneath she's repressing a barrel of anger. I've tried but I get nowhere." We talked about who among us ought to make the effort to reach Theresa. The straw fell to me.

That day I visited Theresa in her hospital room. She had been brought to the hospice unit from her home because she needed more care than we could provide. I asked her if I could come by for a real visit about 8:45 that evening. She agreed with surprising alacrity. Midevening is a good time in hospitals for visits of that character. Visitors are gone. It's often a quiet time for the nurses to take coffee breaks and update charts. The patients are not quite ready for sleep. The medication trolley is being prepared. The noisy hordes of day services are folded up for the night. No one is taking pulses, blood pressure, or temperature. If the TV is on, the volume is low out of deference to those who are preparing for sleep.

So, at the appointed time I pulled up a chair beside Theresa's bed. I let down one bed rail. She held my hand. "Theresa, all of us on the hospice team have become your wildest fans. We are all crazy about you, but we feel there is a lot inside you need to get out if you can. Why carry around a lot of garbage if you don't need to?"

It was a tender moment. She took a big breath, and for the next two hours she poured out a long story of bitter resentment over her ex-husband's lack of support for her children, their needs, their schooling, their housing. She had done it all. Their small attractive home was her doing. The children had been well cared for. Their schooling was well underway. It had been work, work, work. She had no help from any quarter. Men had come into her life, but they had no interest in sharing the responsibility for her family. All they wanted was sex. There was one particular relation that decimated her. The betrayal was still fresh in her tears as she told me about it.

After an hour I became alarmed. She was breathing with difficulty. I suggested we could meet at the same time the next evening, but she would have none of it. "I want to get it all out now while I have the courage," she said. And so she did. When she came to the end, she relaxed on her pillow. I handed her the tissue box. She blew her nose and dried her tears. "There, that's done!" she said.

"Yes," I answered. "Except we need now to give it to God, don't you think?"

"Yes, yes, let's do that!"

I took my oil stock from my pocket and unscrewed it. I always add a tincture of wintergreen to the holy oil. I dipped my finger into the stock and made the sign of the cross upon her forehead and said, "Theresa, I make the sign of Christ's suffering love upon you, and I declare that you are forgiven! His love has received your hurt and the pain of your soul. Go in peace. Your faith has made you whole."

We embraced. I said good night and promised to stick my head in her door the next morning. When I did so, she motioned to me rapidly to come to her side. I said, "How did the night go?" "Oh, Joe, it was wonderful. I haven't had a night of peace like that since I don't know when, and guess what? I could smell his forgiveness all night long!"

After Theresa died, I had the same experience I have had with your Alan, Mary. She came to me with the same smile she had that morning at the hospital except that it was a smile of purest wonder and joy, just like Alan's, which I told you about last week.

So, Mary dear, know that Alan is trying to reach you in your hours of lostness. All is most emphatically well with him. Trust it. Your faith will be a candle in the dark window of your soul leading him to your heart.

Talk to him as naturally as if he were in his favorite chair beside you. Make it as casual and natural as you can. Soon you will have the feeling of a happy nearness, urging you to claim all possible joy that life has yet to give you. The love of Christ gives us graces like that all the time if we let him.

Come see us soon.

With my love,

Joe +

Dear Edward,

Since my last visit with you at the hospital, I have felt a strong need to write a long letter to you about some of the many things we have talked about.

Above all, I must tell you how moved I am by your suffering, and I want to be sure you know how profound my admiration is for the way you are handling your battle with AIDS.

I am filled with wonder by your determination to persevere with appropriate treatment. Although you have repeatedly faced the enormity of your problem, you continue to explore every possible avenue of remission, whether it is a macrobiotic diet or vitamins or chemotherapy or psychological conditioning or spiritual power or experimental medication.

You frequently telephone your friends to stay in touch with the world you know best and to claim their support. You refuse to cop out and pretend that the world has passed you by. In spite of your weakness and fever, you insist on watching the news, on reading. You reach for any food that can help you to gain back some weight. You try to exercise

each day, even if it is only for five or ten minutes. I see all
this and I am awed by your courage.

You also have my unqualified respect for the way you
have stepped up to the issue of how you contracted this
disease. I felt like someone had hit me in the pit of my
stomach when you told me you were reasonably certain
about how you got it. You blamed yourself for not being
more intelligent about your sexual behavior at the time.
You knew about the danger of AIDS, but it was not as
prevalent then as it is now, and the consequences were not
as lethally clear.

I have seldom known anyone who is as balanced as you
are about the cause of a life-threatening illness, especially
when that cause can be traced to another person. You tell
me you were just as responsible as the other party, and that
there is no point in wallowing any more in guilt and blame.
You often say, "Let's get on with the treatment." How
long did you wallow, Edward? We weren't in touch at that
early period of the illness. I shudder to think what you must
have gone through on that issue. You are marvelous in the
way you claim all the help you can get. I wasn't in the least
surprised when you told me what you said at your last
session of the Sloan-Kettering group. Instead of allowing
the period to be overwhelmed by the imminence of death,
you fought back. You hoisted a banner of battle. "Fight the
disease," you pled. "There is help out there. I've tried
acupuncture. It relieves some of my symptoms. I am about
to join a spiritual healing group. I know it will make a
difference. If you aren't happy about the quality of medical
attention you are getting, do something about it. I'm
lucky. I have one of the most supportive and caring

physicians in the city. There are a lot of great people around us, sharing our plight. Find one of them. If you aren't getting the kind of love and understanding from your family you wish you had, change it or accept it. There's plenty of kindness and love right in this group if you ask for it. Again, I'm lucky. My family is great. They are generous and loving. I haven't felt rejected by one of them, and I have two very special friends who spend loads of time with me when I need them, day and night. I think the key to my good luck is that I don't mind asking for good things.''

I can hear you saying every one of those words. They come from an Edward I know and love. Yet, you and I know there is another Edward, the Edward who can be drawn toward the black hole of final despair when the disease throws you into the hospital, gasping for a single breath, as it did only a few weeks ago. Nonetheless, only eight days later you were listening to tapes of positive meditation and faith!

I am overcome when I think of your journey, Edward. We both know that however brave your battle against the disease is, it is still one of the most severe forms of anguish anyone can experience. First there was your awareness that you were different sexually from anyone else in your family and from anyone with whom you grew up. Those years before you declared your sexual identity as an irreversible fact must have been years of intense loneliness and unspeakable confusion. We all yearn to belong, but your belonging was under the judgment of the majority. At the beginning you can only have felt surrounded by an icy circle of isolation. Thank God for the peace you fought for within yourself as time went by, and thank God for the wide circle of friends in which you have moved for the past ten years.

Having AIDS now must be a repeat of those early years.
Once more you are afflicted with a stigma that sets you
apart; only this time the stigma carries with it the dreadful
burden of our society's panic and phobia about the disease.
You are not only not accepted for your sexual orientation,
but you are feared as a carrier of death! Yet, you manage to
maintain a consistent attitude of compassion and
understanding! I recall being with you when you were
buying some necessities at a grocery store. Your appearance
fits the image so many of us have of the AIDS-afflicted
patient; people suspect your condition at first glance. You
simply ignored all those looks of hostility as we moved
through the grocery store, babbling away to me about a
play you had seen recently on Broadway. How have you
escaped the debilitating effects of feeling victimized,
Edward? I have seen you angry and repulsed by the attitudes
of the public, but it never lasts. You often say, "I can't
afford to waste energy on being angry about the public
outcry."

However, Edward, what I really want to write about
has to do with the two deepest relations of your life. I am
thinking about your relation to your mother and your
relation to your soul.

You have been superb in your effort of affirming all the
positives you could find in your life, and in a general face-
saving way you have also handled your relation to your
mother with much grace, in spite of many scratchy
incidents along the way these tough two years. Underneath
your style of courtesy, however, I have sensed a deep need in
you to have your mother's love and approval, and I have felt

your anger over the absence of that support in the way that you desire it. I feel your anger is like a lion in chains. Edward, you can't help what you feel. Don't apologize for your feelings, but let's get them on the table with your mother! All of us aim our fire against those who are dearest to us when we are hurting badly.

It is clear to me that the most conflictual aspect of your life is your love for your mother. I have talked with her at length about your condition, as you well know. Most of your life in the past twelve years has been led apart from her. I doubt if she knows even five percent of your experience in that time. I'm sure you know that she made her peace with your sexual orientation long ago. It was not easy for her, nor did it happen without much anguish and excessive self-accusation. Yet, at no time did she reject you or try to inflict a burden of guilt upon you for your sexuality. It was over a year before she came to be comfortable and truly accepting of it after your disclosure. However, some parents of gay progeny never get to that point.

I appeal to you, Edward, to trust me when I tell you that your mother loves you profoundly. Stand on that solid reality. Share your honest feeling with her gently, quietly. Blame is not the name of the game. It ruins everything. Both you and your mother have fought enough inner battles with your natures to know that emotions are prodigiously complex when they are as deep as they are between the two of you.

On some of my visits with you, I see your low levels of energy, the constant problems of food and diet, the daily struggle with symptoms of the disease, and yet through it I perceive a long repressed rebellion against your mother coming to the surface. You are asking something from her that she is unable to give. She tells me her response is one of unutterable confusion. She feels the intensity of your need, but she is blocked by something in your spirit from giving you what you want. The result is abysmal distress. She wants to love you and reassure you, but she is overwhelmed by an atmosphere of conflict and barely submerged hostility.

She tells me that no matter what she says, you contradict her. Your experience has made you exceptionally knowledgeable about gourmet food, the theatre, dance, cinema, and various luminaries in the entertainment world. Your mother's experience in that milieu is nonexistent. So, naturally, you speak with an authority in those fields that she cannot match. You often treat her as though she were your own age if not even younger than you are.

There is a decision I beg you to make, Edward. The journey of the soul is everlastingly determined by our choices. It begins with us and it ends with us. For your soul's sake I beseech you to finish this unfinished business with your mother. Find a way to be open and honest with her. Don't give up until the relation is reconciled. Your soul will be mended by that gift. Without it, you will find yourself in a straitjacket of the spirit on the other side, whenever that time comes, unable to move, stuck in a painful isolation of the soul, pleading for the angels of God to release you. Time is radically different in the next world, where we have no choice but to confront the truth about ourselves. Primal relations that are unfinished here have the gravest consequences there.

You may ask what I mean by soul making. It all

revolves around our being. Doing, believing, thinking, feeling, willing, are only facets of our being. As I write about this great mystery, I realize I am writing not only about your soul's pilgrimage but mine as well. It is ever thus. None of us is so unique as to be exempt from the human condition.

One day I went to Amsterdam to visit the Vincent Van Gogh Museum. One particular portrait arrested me. It was the face of a very old man. His eyes had the look of someone who has seen all there is to see in the cruelty and the violence of human experience. His torn and weathered brown cap sat squarely on his head. His face was lined with creases of infinite sadness. A cry of profound tragedy came from his mouth. The words I heard from him were "Attention. Pay attention." It was a plea from the other side of the abyss, a voice from the eternal. I stood transfixed by the power and intensity of the portrait. A line of Buddhist wisdom came to me, "Be a lamp unto thyself." The man in the portrait was begging me to be more serious about my destiny. He was telling me that everything hangs upon the seriousness and integrity with which we persevere in the journey of the soul.

I do not know by what grace I have been given three score and almost ten years, but I bend my knees in humble gratitude for that grace. The time that is given to each of us is a mystery. Had I died when I was thirty, I would have been so unformed a soul as scarcely to know who I was in the presence of the angels of mercy. Had I died when I was forty, my wounded ego, which I had concealed from everyone, would have held me in its tenacious grip through eternity. Had I died when I was sixty, things done and things left undone, the power of guilt, and the neglect of my soul's destiny would have barred the path of my soul's freedom.

But by the grace of God I have been given the incomparable gift of time—time to listen, time to be alone, time to bleed and time to heal, time to be silent, and time to wait. With T.S. Eliot I can at last say to my soul without shame and without fear, "Be still and let the dark come upon you—which shall be the darkness of God."

To think you have had only three decades to work out your destiny terrifies me, but, dear man, you have the golden gift of knowledge of the end. At thirty, I had no reason to think that the world was not my oyster, but had I seriously thought I might die before my next birthday, I would have welcomed into my life anyone who could have helped me to prepare for the next sphere. By thirty, I had dealt with the mystery of death through the tragedy of warfare, as well as in my family.

I knew even then that the sure hope for my soul was through an identification with the boundless, awesome energy that entered the stream of human consciousness through Christ. The evolution of human consciousness was profoundly altered by those "three sad days" from Good Friday to Easter. No teacher, however great, no human being, however gifted, could have achieved that alteration. Only a divine intervention, releasing a God-filled impulse of immeasurable power, could have accomplished that change in the tide of history.

Although I could not have verbalized my experience of Christ in those words when I was thirty, I would have recognized the truth of them, and I would have made it my business to know his will for me in the time I had left on this planet. Each person's time, each lifetime, short or long or in between, is finally none other than this—the crucible in which we shape and reshape, form and re-form, the soul we bring back to the source from which we come. There is no greater grace to assist us in that shaping than the Christ impulse that streams into our soul's consciousness when we open ourselves to him.

The pattern of your essential self is woven by the threads of all that you have desired and loved, of all that you have done, believed, thought, felt, and willed since you were born. As long as you breathe, those threads continue to weave and reweave the pattern of the person you are. There is no escape from the process. It goes on whether you recognize it or deny it. Most of the process remains hidden in the depths of the unconscious. At the core of the process there is an essential you that is continuously evolving in response to the impact of daily experience. We, in religion, call that developing essential person the soul.

Its character, its form, its shape, is our responsibility. It is overwhelmingly the most important task to which we are called in life. I used to think parenthood was the greatest responsibility we ever carry. I know now that, although it is an awesome calling, parenthood is but for a season. Even a parent cannot ultimately be responsible for his child. I have often thought, too, that I was deeply responsible for the people to whom I have given my heart in love. I know now that, although we bear one another's burdens in love, and so fulfill the law of Christ, in the final accounting I cannot be responsible for another person's soul.

I have often wondered what is meant by the text "It is a

fearful thing to fall into the hands of the Living God.''
Now in my later years I think I know. When I pass beyond
the gate of death I will fall into the hands of the Living God,
and I, only I, will be responsible for the core of the person I
bring into his fields of praise.

If I have never seriously thought about my inner being,
if I have lived always on the surface of things with no
attention to the values that sustain our individual and
common life, if I have consistently refused to deal with the
great questions of creation and destiny, of beginnings and
endings, if I have made no effort to understand myself and
the pattern of my reactions to people, if I have avoided any
insight into the reasons for my behavior and my
misbehavior, if I have lived so superficially that I have
always been running, running, running away from the
harsh problems and realities of primal suffering and social
injustice, then I shall know what a fearful thing it is to fall
into the hands of the Living God because I will have
nothing to bring him except a thin veil of confused images,
signifying nothing but wasted opportunities.

There is another level I have pondered, Edward, and it
revolves around the problem of authority. If I have never
accepted any authority greater than myself, if I have
regularly put my own will ahead of any other consideration,
if I have avoided a commitment to that which deserves my
reverence and veneration, if I consistently preferred my own
pleasures and fulfillment to any other interest, if I have
regarded speech as something to be used for personal gain
and recognition regardless of truth, if I have used other
people for my own gain and satisfaction with little thought
for their rights and privileges, if I have betrayed the trust
that others have reposed in me by breaking their confidences

or by countless hypocrisies and double-talk, then when I pass the gate of death, I shall know what a fearful thing it is to fall into the hands of the Living God, because I will have nothing to bring him but an empty cup, a chalice he gave me at birth into which I have poured nothing worth saving.

We become the persons we are by the things to which we belong. If we have never belonged to anything but ourselves, then we have only empty selves to bring to the Living God when the end comes. The nobler, the higher, the greater our commitments, the more and more we become the persons God intended us to be. It took me a long time in life to learn in my inward being a truth I heard years and years ago. At last I well know that my being has but one supreme law: I want to belong to Christ as deeply, as utterly as possible, because I know it is only in belonging to him that I have and hope of becoming the person he made me to be; without him I have only an empty cup to bring to the Living God.

But we have not yet touched bottom. It is not the mind, nor the will, but the heart that counts in the end. If I harbor a resentment against anyone, if I look back on my life and blame someone else's inadequacy for my deprivations, if I persist in thinking of myself as a victim, a helpless pawn moved about on the complicated chessboard of life's fortuitous circumstances and accidents, manipulated by those who should have known better, betrayed by those I loved and respected, perhaps even rejected by God, if I refuse the grace of forgiveness, forgiving, and being forgiven, then when I come to the moment of ultimate and inescapable truth, naked and exposed to the full glare of divine reality, I shall find the gates closed.

To refuse to forgive is to reject the other person as that

person is. As we forgive, so we are forgiven. As we refuse to forgive, so we are unforgiven. Kierkegaard wrote, "I must have faith that God in forgiving has forgotten what guilt there is—in thinking of God I must think that he has forgotten it, and to learn to dare to forget it myself in forgiveness."

I beg you to dare to forget the barriers of guilt and anger of the past, knowing that if God can forget them, you can, too! Don't misunderstand, beloved man; the barriers are better faced before they are forgotten. I am one of those who took an unconscionable length of time to learn that wisdom; but once faced, openly, truly, and worked out as best you can with those who may be involved in the tangle of your life, there comes a moment when you "must have faith that God in forgiving has forgotten," and in that hour of Godlight forgive and forget yourself.

When I started this letter I had just visited the hospital. I looked at your eyes, glazed with fatigue. I hugged you and kissed your brow. Your head was wet with fevered perspiration. I came down here to my little study near the ocean. I unlocked the door and wept. I wish I could give you more than the comfort of my life, and I guess it is that driving need in me to help you that made me bold enough to write this long, windy letter. I can only add that I believe in miracles, and I believe in that courageous spirit of yours. It may even yet win the day!

As always,

J.

My dear Helen,

This morning I woke up full of anxiety for you and Edward. By the time I had showered, shaved, and had my coffee, I was beginning to suspect my fears were only hobgoblins of the night. However, I could not rest until I had called the hospital. I asked for that nice nurse when I got the nurses' station on the phone. She assured me there had been no significant change in Edward's condition since last I talked with her.

After that, I decided to have a morning pipe of tobacco. As I sat in my hideaway study talking with the Lord, it came to me that my dreams of last night centered on you. The burden of my night consciousness seemed to be that you were in extreme conflict and some stupid barrier was preventing me from reaching you in my dream. The phone was dead. The car made a pathetic click when I turned on the ignition. The battery was dead. I panicked. Death was all around me. I feared you were dying. "No," I said to myself, "it must be Edward." Upon reflection this morning, I realized my fears about you were as groundless as were my fears about Edward. After all, we had just talked to one another last evening about Edward's progress and treatment. I realized I had to sort out my impressions and anxieties about you and Edward and myself. The best way I know to do that is to write you one of my windy, weighty epistles!

Homosexuality is a hopelessly complex maze. I have long since given up trying to understand it. The more I read about it, the longer I reflect about it; the deeper I look at my own sexual history, the less I think I know about it. It has been the same story when I have studied the whole field of human sexuality. My psychiatric training has given me some priceless handles, but even those insights are woefully inadequate for the task. I look with wonder and awe at lecturers in medical schools and seminaries for whom sex is a well-charted hemisphere whose geography is described with ease and authority. I wish I could follow its tortuous ravines and mountainous heights as confidently as they do. Frustration even makes me envy my moral and conservative friends for whom sex is an open-and-shut case between that which is sinful and that which is not. For them, one kind of sex is right and one is wrong. They don't see the complexities and contradictions, the inconsistencies and surprises, the repressions and sufferings that I have seen in well over forty years of listening to the abysmal pain of countless persons as they have shared the intimate dimensions of their experience with me. Or perhaps I am wrong. Maybe they see just as much as I do but are more clearly guided than I am to know what God approves of and what he does not. Perhaps I shouldn't be so afraid of making judgments. When it comes to sex, the world of judgment is a terrifying mine field to me. There is so much I don't know, I feel compelled to surrender it all to the mercy of God. He knows; I don't.

Yet there is no escape from the issues. We all live with them and we all have to deal with the consequences of our sexuality and of those we love. Edward's sexual choices have brought you untold pain, but I know you also recognize that his sexual identity has brought him untold joy and fulfillment. I say this in spite of the tragic shadow the affliction of AIDS now casts over him, as well as yourself. A middle-aged friend turned his anguished face to me years ago when he was telling me about his inability to relate to women on an intimate level and asked, ''So what am I to do, Joe? Am I to go on the rest of my life denied of any closeness or intimacy with another human being?'' I cannot fail to be grateful that such anguish has not been Edward's fate.

Your response is very likely ''Well, I'd rather he had the anguish of loneliness, even isolation, than AIDS.'' But ten or fifteen years ago we never knew there was such a thing as AIDS. Had that been the case, it is at least conceivable that Edward might have chosen a different life-style if not a heterosexual identity.

It rends my heart. I wish we were sitting together this moment. Silence and tears seem the only appropriate way to meet this tragedy. Words slip and slide off the jagged face of this mountainous sorrow.

Yet I must persevere. You have raised concerns and questions that I am bound to address. I cannot say ''answer'' because anything I might say in the presence of so great a grief is inevitably tentative stammering.

You were understandably desolated by Edward's

diagnosis. I wonder if anything in your previous experience could compare to it. You have stolen several marches on destiny, and now death and tragedy have caught up with you. Not many of us escape those looming figures for over six decades of life. Yet, my beloved friend, in spite of little preparation for it I must say you are carrying this grievous burden like a veteran.

I can hear your voice in quick repudiation of my admiration. I know you think you aren't meeting this challenge at all well. Just recently you wrote me, "I thought I had accepted Edward's homosexuality, but now I realize I hadn't made as much progress as I thought I had achieved. My early background of conservative Christianity came upon me with a vengeance when I realized Edward had AIDS. I'm shocked at myself. You won't believe me, but it's true. I really had a moment of terror when it came over me: I saw Edward's illness as God's righteous judgment and punishment for being a homosexual! What do you think that means? At some unconscious level, do you suppose I must really think that?"

Perhaps you may, my dear Helen, but we have to remember there is a difference between thinking a thing and acting upon it. For many people who are driven by their emotions, there is little interruption between thought and action, but you are not one of them. Your natural reserve protects you from acting out your impulses. Don't hold yourself responsible for your thoughts. We can't help what we think. Thoughts are like a multitude of winging birds. The old adage is still relevant: "We may not be responsible for the birds that fly over our heads, but we can keep them from making a nest in our hair."

That is what you have done. Edward feels himself wholly supported by you. He told me in a note the other day that he had made his peace with you during those weeks of remission he spent with you last winter. You well know how welcome that news was to me! Yet I also realize it would take Edward at least two years of sharp-bladed therapy to resolve the complexities and conflicts he carries in his relation to you. Both you and I know there isn't time for that now, nor is it appropriate. He needs all his energy to meet the silent monster in his bloodstream.

Meanwhile, he feels accepted by you for the brave, courageous, interesting, and fun person he is, and he certainly has no impression whatever that you think he is under the finger of divine judgment. In fact, I'm sure it is your quiet faithfulness to your Christian commitment that has recently sent him back to church in search of a spiritual director. No matter what horrendous thoughts and conflicts you may have had, the crucial point is that your actions, your behavior, have conveyed to him an impression of acceptance, support, and love. I do not think for a minute that there has been even a shadow of insincerity in what you have said to or done for Edward. Judge yourself by what you have intended toward him, not by what your unconscious throws up on the screen of your mind. If you will give yourself some modicum of credit in this long tunnel, you will see that you have done what any reasonable person could ask of you at your present stage in dealing with Edward.

Nevertheless, I feel there is a question still hanging in the background. I suspect your rational and sensible self is in essential agreement with me about Edward's understanding of your acceptance of him. You are asking something that is beneath what you have said and done to Edward. I hear you telling me that you are ashamed of having a son who is a homosexual and that you aren't proud of those feelings. Perhaps I would be closer to the mark if I said simply that you are still unresolved in your feelings about homosexuality, especially for someone close to you. There is a buried doubt in you about the issue that AIDS has resurrected, isn't there?

It doesn't cut much mustard, does it, for me to say that you are in good company. I don't know any parent of a homosexual son or a lesbian daughter who is a missionary for the cause, or eager to convert friends to positive acceptance. Nor do I know a parent who has won, an open and genuine peace about the issue.

There is nothing as beautiful as the union of a man and a woman whose love is mutual and whose commitment to one another is profound and faithful. Such intimacy is the symbol of all human yearning. The law of opposites is suspended; the polarity is banished if only for a few moments. When the fulfillment of that hunger for unity is grounded in a marriage of mind and heart, it becomes a covenant that can only be likened to the bond by which Christ has faithfully united himself to his church for two thousand years.

Helen, it has taken me a long time to see that same beauty in a commitment of similar depth and faithfulness between two people of the same sex.

The oceanic proportions of this subject defeat me. I have read a dozen books about it, to say nothing of the Bible. The overriding authority in my life is Scripture. The texts in

Genesis, Leviticus, Romans, have held me in their sway for many years. However, the longer I reflect on those texts as applied to same sex commitments, the harder it is for me to believe they are in conformity with the figure of the Gospels. Not all scripture is equally authoritative. When I bring the persons I love, whose sexual identity differs from the majority of us, into the presence of Christ, I find nothing but compassion. Is it conceivable that Christ would reject someone who was born with a genetic predisposition that deviates from the so-called norm? I find it beyond my conception. If his love welcomes such persons, shouldn't we? There is no prayer I would wish to see answered in Edward's life in this stage of his journey so much as my prayer that he might know how high, how broad, how deep, how unconditional, Christ's love is for him.

It is stretching wildly to think that there could be a positive in the plague of AIDS, but I do see one. Might it not compel the homosexual community to accept the same standards of virginity and faithfulness as we have traditionally expected of the heterosexual population? Much of the promiscuity and the sleazy side of the homosexual life-style are a mirror of the phobias and fantasies in which Western culture has seen the phenomenon. Perhaps AIDS would be an alarm clock calling *all* of us to a commitment of reserve and faithfulness in the conduct of our intimate lives? I know when Edward plays the tortuous "if only" game in his mind during the long nights of loneliness, he wishes with all his heart that he might have had the good fortune and the wisdom to have found a partner years ago to whom he could have made a life commitment.

I must be careful not to oversimplify. We both know

that human sexuality, homosexual and heterosexual, is endlessly complex. The reasons for a multitude of deviations, obsessions, compulsions, fixations, fetishes, fears, impotencies, promiscuities, images, fantasies, and practices are appallingly complicated. As soon as we isolate one cause for one aspect of our sexual history, the thing is like mercury. It slips from our grasp, and we recognize that the explanation is only a fraction of the answer. The insights of Freud are indispensable to any understanding, but no responsible therapist of my acquaintance claims adequacy for Freudian thought in this area any more. I wonder if we will ever fully understand the labyrinthine twists and paths of our sexual needs.

My dear Helen, the observation is relevant. I know you have lain awake in the early morning hours asking yourself if you are to blame for Edward's sexual preferences. There was an uncommon closeness between yourself and Edward throughout his early years. You have told me how concerned you were about that dependency, even when he was ten and twelve years of age. You have also turned over in your mind dozens of times what connection there might be in Edward's development between the image of a self-defeating and unsuccessful father and Edward's rejection of the male role in life.

Believe me, it is a futile pursuit. No one knows for sure what these connections might be. After all, Edward's brothers are happily adjusted heterosexual males, and you were also deeply involved with their growing years. I have counseled many homosexual men whose fathers were among the most successful and balanced people I know. They were clearly heterosexual, virile men, engaged in typical male pursuits. I have also known the mothers of homosexuals who strongly encouraged their sons to be independent, assuming responsibility for their own lives at appropriate stages of development. I have known lesbians whose mothers were distant, cold, and rejecting. I have also known lesbian women whose mothers were the perfect images of cuddly warmth and consistent lovingness. I have known lesbian women whose fathers were among the most caring of persons, and I have known others whose fathers were remembered mainly for their unavailability. I have known many homosexual persons in whose families there was no memory whatsoever of homosexual members, and I have known some in whose family history there was a recollected impression of homosexual preference. Previous generations put a tight cover over such people, as you know.

I recite this history of experience because it illustrates better than theory can, how vain it is to draw conclusions about this phenomenon. It is wiser and kinder to all of us who are involved with homosexual progeny to face the complexity and admit that we don't really know the answers. Blaming ourselves only compounds the problem. I wish society at large were as compassionate about the problem, but that can't be helped. The twenty-first century will see broad changes in attitudes toward homosexuality, but you and I will not live to see that day. In the meantime, we have to make our peace with it as responsibly as we can.

I have dwelt on Edward's homosexuality, Helen, because I cannot escape the feeling that you won't handle his dreadful illness adequately until you have settled your mind about his sexual preference. The two are inseparable.

When you refuse to deal with one side of the coin, it automatically follows that you will not deal with the other side either. The whole thing gets tucked away. When you become comfortable with his homosexuality, you will see his battle with AIDS as no different than any cherished young friend's mortal combat—let us say with cancer of the liver. Society sees a difference, but that needn't matter to you once you have passed the taboo of homosexuality.

He needs you, and you need him. He needs your love in an abundant measure. He is incredibly brave, but behind his eyes I see a monster of fear. You are wonderful in the way you have given him your reassurance and emotional support. Persevere with it in greater and greater measure. The authentic depth of your caring will comfort him more than anything anyone can give him.

When this is all over, I covet for you the feeling that Edward died in the knowledge that your presence was given to him without reserve, and I yearn for you to have the comfort of knowing you gave him all that you could give him. Guilt pounces on us with its heavy, hot-clawed feet after the death of a child, a spouse, a parent, before the ground is green above their graves. I long for you to be protected from its attack.

Please don't allow what I have asked of you to lay too heavily upon your heart. I beg you not to feel that you must achieve more tolerance or to give more love than you can command naturally, but I know you well enough to know that your natural generosity flows with great ease once you have settled thorny issues in your mind. Feeling can't be forced, but it can be blocked unneedfully. There is a bottomless reservoir of devotion to Edward in your soul. It simply waits upon your wholehearted assent before it flows naturally and fully from you to him. Let it happen in its own way and in its own time. Your soul will be blessed by it, and his will too.

Do please know that I think of you and Edward in my prayers every day.

With my love,

J.+

My dear David,

I walked into that rather low-ceilinged, barren, dusty chapel in the Unitarian church at Harvard Square, forty-five minutes before your father's memorial service was to begin. My purpose in going so early was twofold. I wanted to have enough time to center myself and to be in touch with my feelings and with the Holy Spirit. I also wanted to have enough time to reach across the miles that separate us and touch your hand. You were abundantly with me, David, throughout the afternoon.

There were purple and red anemones at the center of the altar. A single candlestick on either side stood silently waiting. Just before the service, the minister in charge came in and lit them from his cigarette lighter. I can't explain to you what those two flickering candles meant to me. Their presence was the most powerful fact of the entire service. They spoke to me. They seemed to say, "I am the light of the world, but my name will not be mentioned today. What I came into the world to do and to suffer will not be acknowledged, nor will my promises be honored; nevertheless, I am here, and the darkness shall not overcome." At the end of the service, I was almost the first one out of the room. I couldn't bear to see those candles snuffed out. Stupid and emotional, wasn't it, but that's the way I felt.

There was a lovely quartet of flute, clarinet, violin, and cello. They entered and played before and after the service as well as in the middle. There were about seventy people, considerably more women than men. Three speakers told of their devotion and admiration for your father. Each tribute to him as an architect and as a person was a perfect gem, beautifully written, urbane, sophisticated, warm, caring, and fully conscious of the mortality none of us escapes. At no point was there an affirmation of grace, forgiveness, inescapable judgment, or any reference to the being and the re-becoming in which you and I believe.

Naturally, I miseed all that, but its presence would have introduced a jarring note of utter phoniness. Your father's integrity required the service to be exactly as it was. The rarified atmosphere of Cambridge was fragrant everywhere. I have experienced it many times in Harvard's cloistered circles, as you have. We Christians are not the only people who are sometimes guilty of an arrogance that presumes to know the answers to the ultimate questions of life's meaning. The secular intellectuals are as presumptuous in thinking there are no ultimate answers as we are in thinking we know it all.

I know how much it troubles you that you were unable to convey to your father the luminous light you and I have come to see with greater and greater glory in Christ, but, David, there was no animating desire in Bob to see what we see. His natural regard for diverse opinion and varied experience compelled him to listen carefully to your words about Christ, and because he had such sincere respect for you as a person, he was eager to hear what you had to say. However, I believe that was as far as it went. The furniture of his mind was so full of secular assumptions, accumulated over a lifetime of skepticism, there was no space for a window in the soul to Christ.

My memories of Bob in Cambridge are legion. I have sat with him by the hour while we spun spider-thin filaments of rationality around the proposition that all creation springs from an original and divine design. As an architect, this line of reasoning elicited a limited response in our theological meanderings, but before the evening was over I knew I had been had. He always managed quietly and skillfully to tilt the argument in his favor, and I even caught a whiff of gentle ridicule in my nostrils as the visit ended. There was a certain satisfaction in that sweet dimpled smile of his as he bade me goodnight.

Our reunions, after brief periods of absence, were invariably warm, mutual, and genuine. Conversation between us, glasses in hand, almost always began at once. Marvelous talk it was. Apart from religion, our commonalities in the fields of politics, social policy, aesthetic standards, fiction, and poetry made our times together a pure pleasure for me. I enjoyed the sheer volume of his mind, its humor, its inclusiveness.

Two of his characteristics remain with me. One was his strong ethical sense, which could express itself in acerbic, finely tuned, withering moral outrage from time to time. I don't think we were ever closer to one another than we were after those trips of mine to Alabama and Mississippi to identify with the civil rights movement. The other was his devotion to his craft as an architect. His imagination was prodigious. His work had true originality. Although he admired Gropius and Frank Lloyd Wright hugely, Bob's work was never imitative. It was his own. His integrity would permit no other result. Somewhere I have a square block of green glass. Bob gave it to me in 1942. It was an example of new building materials he was excited about. He loved frontiers in the world of art, as well as science. When his brother Fitz became deeply involved with the nuclear scientists who tried to warn us of what was to come after Hiroshima, there was a part of Bob that desperately wanted to share that fight; but he couldn't find his niche in the politics of it at the time. Although, I remember his excitement over lunch at the Wursthaus regarding the report from the Club of Rome that first began to alert us to the limits of science as an instrument of civilized existence.

Morality and esthetics, and what else? There, I'm afraid, I stop; except I have to say that I also have memories of his shadow: his irritability, his unjustified anger, his depressions, and, in one period of his life, his obsessive, irrational, out-of-control jealousy. Truth also compels me to say that he was quite capable of unfeeling cruelty from time to time.

That's as far as my memory takes me. Circumstances conspired to change things between Bob and myself. Carola's illness began to approach an acute stage. Your parents were divorced. I was increasingly immersed in my work, and in all the complexities of my over-full life.

Carola's cancer became more and more absorbing of my energies as her husband. I heard nothing from Bob. The communication lines had been cut.

When Carola was in college she fell in love with Bob, but by then he was bedazzled by the irresistible charm and beauty and radiance of your mother. I doubt if he did more than indulge Carola's devotion to him in a sort of avuncular fashion. Still, there was a bond between them. Her braininess, unbending integrity, moral commitments, and aesthetic interests matched his at many points. I used to wonder if it ever occurred to him that he had married the wrong Franchot girl. I think she would have liked to have heard from him before she died.

In any case, after the divorce and Bob's marriage to Mary, I was not in touch with your father again until a week ago in that dingy chapel in Cambridge. Lately, he has been with me in more ways than I can explain.

I keep wondering what Bob must be experiencing now. You told me that moments before he died he lifted his arms upward as though he were about to be embraced by someone who was waiting for him to arrive. Who knows? He wrote of his gratitude to you for your letter about the essentiality of Christ as "the means of grace and hope of glory." It is conceivable, in that long Herculean battle of his with cancer, he thought quietly and privately and deeply about your faith and your plea for a commitment to the good news of Christ. Isn't it possible that his arms were lifted toward the God of compassion we call Jesus? For now, David, we have to content ourselves with an "I don't know." But we can hope, can't we?

Where are you, David, in your thinking about

individual resurrection? Teilhard Le Chardin's insights about an evolving universe and the power of consciousness to prepare us for a new stage in the evolution of humanity have left a deep imprint on my faith. Outside my study window I have just glanced at a scattering of boulders and rocks strewn along our shoreline. There is one huge stone behind our house in which there is a cleft that forms a perfect place in which to sit in the afternoon sun. Last summer, my seven-year-old grandchild sat in that hollowed place as though the gods had dropped her there from the sky. I thought the rock rather liked the feeling of the child's warmth on its bosom. What a contrast it was, though, when she stood up, hopped to the top, danced on one foot, and ran down the hill.

Some springs ago, I picked up a swallow from our lawn. I thought she was dead. However, as soon as I held the feathered creature in the warmth of my cupped hands I felt her heart beating a hundred times a second. She seemed to be lamed and exhausted after flying thousands of miles to return to her northern nest. The day was warm, and after I had held her a while I gently laid her in the protection of that same rock. An hour later I saw her hobbling about tentatively. She turned her head to the east and the west, and before I could step toward her she was off into the air and beyond my sight.

This winter I was walking in our woods. We all know that if you want to connect with the creatures of the forest there must come a time when you simply rest and remain perfectly still. I chose a special tree on the path that I prize. It is just an ancient maple, whose shade in the summer is like an umbrella against the sun. During the autumn its leaves are a glory to behold. Since no one rakes the forest, and few people walk in it, the leaves beneath its crown and trunk are plentiful and soft.

I remained under the fanlike shape of the leafless tree for some time. Then I heard a twig break. Slowly I turned my head in the direction of the sound, only to be electrified by the eye contact of a magnificent buck deer, standing in a crevice of the woods beside a brook. What a noble, massive creature he was. Alas, no sooner had I lifted my binoculars for a better glimpse of him than he was gone, bounding across the brook and through the brush.

Such different bodies, David! The rock, the tree, the deer, the bird, the child. Each physical being seems to be in the service of a new and higher consciousness. Stage by stage, inertia, weight, bondage, muteness, are overcome. At each level there is greater and greater freedom, an increase of lightness, scope, movement, resourcefulness. Matter more and more becomes permeated by the spirit, until in the human body the spirit finds a fullness of expression that is positively awesome.

Could it not be, David, that when the "word became flesh" and dwelt among us "full of grace and truth," "made in all ways like unto ourselves," we saw not only a revelation of the mystery of God but also a revelation of the mystery of our own making and our own destiny?

Are not St. Paul's words pure visions of truth? "Now some man will say how do the dead rise again! What manner of body shall they become? That which thou sowest is not quickened is it unless it die? And that which thou sowest is not the body which shall be, but bare grain—God giveth it a body as he will—to every seed its proper body.

All flesh is not the same. One is the flesh of men, another of beasts, another of birds. And there are bodies celestial and bodies terrestrial, but one is the glory of the sun, another the glory of the moon, and another the glory of the stars, for one star differeth from another star in glory. So, also, is the resurrection of the dead. Man's body is sown in corruption, it shall rise in incorruption. It is sown in dishonor, it shall rise in glory. It is sown in weakness, it shall rise in power. It is sown a natural body, it shall rise a spiritual body. As we have borne the image of the earthly in us let us also bear in ourselves the image of the heavenly.''

However, between the earthly image, the physical body, and the heavenly image, the spiritual body, there is the inevitable reality of death. I have come to believe, David, that the heavenly image is not something we are given. We grow toward it. All of our life, in this world or the next, we either grow toward it or we grow away from it. No life can be evaluated until it is over. If that is true in human terms, it must be true in heavenly terms.

David, I lean with all my strength upon the commitment I have made to Christ to save me in the life and the judgment that are to come. I know I shall not be some speck of light added to his divine brilliance, nor some drop of mercy added to the ocean of his love, nor some memory recorded in my family's history. I shall be real, and I shall inescapably be the very person I have at last become at the moment of my death. When I say I believe in the resurrection of the body, I mean that I believe in the resurrection of my personhood, the personhood of every human being.

What becomes of us when we come into the sphere of

judgment and truth? God's grace, his forgiveness, his unconditional love, make all things possible to those who believe, even purification and preparation for our continued journey toward Christ. Those texts in the New Testament about judgment are not meaningless. Grace doesn't cancel out all that was done on earth. What becomes of the wilfulness with which we resisted the claims of purity and justice? What about a person whose whole life is riddled with the ravages of wrongdoing? When we move into the sphere of the next world, beyond the bliss of knowing we are not dead but alive in a world of inexpressible spiritual power, what happens to us? God is unblemished holiness. How do we unholy ones move toward that world of untouchable splendor? I cannot escape the conclusion that we proceed only by a process of purification and suffering. We gradually experience ourselves as we are in truth, and in that realization there is a divine fire that purifies us. We are penetrated by that cleansing flame until we are in a state of readiness for communion with the Eternal.

In this process of dying and living again we are caught up in a terrifying mystery. The pain and growth that was refused must be learned. The truth we would not face must be confronted. The betrayal of love must be overcome. Pride, vanity, evasion, indifference, are gone. We find ourselves on the side of truth against ourselves. In the midst of that mysterious suffering the heart submits to the power and love of the Holy Spirit that makes us new creatures in Christ, participants in the glory of the new creation, citizens of the new Jerusalem.

Well, David, I have rambled on and on, but your father's death started a long train of thought in my heart. I wanted to share it with you. Your submission to the authority of Scripture and to the lordship of Christ puts us on common ground, and I want you to tell me where you think I have missed the mark in writing about your father whom I greatly admired.

Write me soon. How is your work going? And the Ph.D.?

> A hug to each of the children,
> love to you and Kay.

Joe ⊕

Dear Raymond,

I want to talk with you about your soul, but of course you must know that in doing so I am also talking about my own soul making. The great universals include all of us.

For many years I have been captured by the text "Except a grain of corn falls into the ground and dies, it remains alone, but if it dies, it bears much fruit." Isn't that the essence of the faith we share? "He that would save his life will lose it, but he who loses his life for my sake shall find it." It is in dying that we live again. Without goodbyes there can be no greetings. Each day is overtaken by the lengthening shadow of night. If it were not so, there would be no tomorrow. All life is a series of little deaths intended to prepare us for the last one.

Your struggle against the dying of the body is truly heroic. There is even something Promethean about it. That iron will of yours refuses to bend. I see you sorely chafed and bruised by your resistance to the disabilities and increasing weaknesses of the flesh.

This resistance confirms my experience. Several people closely connected to me fought the oncoming of death with a similar ferocity. Like you, they were persons of enormous willpower and unbending integrity, imbued with an unswerving loyalty to their commitments. They were gifted with an unusually keen sensitivity to the differences between practice and pretension. They loathed phoniness and officiousness. They heard the voice of conscience as clearly as I hear the croaking of the Canadian geese on their return flight in early springtime.

They were also persons who exercised great control in many directions. Lately, I have wondered if the fear of death might not have been a deep and submerged part of their impressive strength and control.

In the case of my first wife, Carola, I am confident that the fear of death and fear of the loss of control were tied to one another. Her all-encompassing preoccupations with the details of treatment, changes of medication, surgical procedures, levels of dosage, second medical opinions, were the natural expressions of her remarkably alert and sophisticated intelligence; but under the intellectualizing that surrounded her last illness, there was clear evidence of her tenacious determination to maintain as much personal control of her destiny as possible. She fought her death until the last gasp. I am certain that her greatest terror was the specter of an absolute loss of control.

I think that has been one of your battles, too, Raymond. You are one of those persons whose strength of character has given abundant evidence of great determination of will. It was all a part of your great success in the corporate world, and one of the reasons for the wonderfully enduring respect in which you continue to be held. When your illness robbed you of freedom of movement and clarity of judgment, your

anger was often at white-hot levels of intensity. You were
not going to give up control of your life without mortal
combat.

But then your sight was taken from you. No treatment
is known by which it can be returned. Was it the
irrevocability of your blindness that finally compelled your
acceptance? Was it the darkness that brought the gift of
peace? Somehow, I have the feeling that when you faced the
inescapable reality of dependence you were released from
your rage. You had no more options. Survival mandated
cooperation. The simplest routines of daily life required the
assistance of other people. From that time on, there has been
a difference. Is it resignation I see on your good strong
features as you sit silently in your chair, waiting for the
lunch tray to come? Is it positive acceptance I see in your
folded hands as you lie on your back, tucked into your bed
for the night, protected by rails on each side? Or is it stoical
endurance, a quiet desperation—awaiting for the end? I
wish I knew. I suspect it is now one, now another, and yet
none of the above.

I long to talk with you about the deep matters of destiny
and the spirit, the way we used to talk when we walked
along the back roads of the farm. I would give anything to
hear your "yes, yes, yes, that's the way life is," or your
deep booming voice saying "no, I don't agree." Now there
is a gulf between us. Our minds no longer meet. The words
won't come. The sentences are full of fuzzy pauses. The
frustration we both experience keeps us from trying again.
A few minutes later it is forgotten and we are left with the
pearly gift of blessedness. The bonds of trust and friendship

remain. In the silence our hearts meet. Presently, we pat one another's hand and I take my leave.

But if we could talk, what would I propose we say to each other? Your soul is so beautifully prepared for the next sphere of being, I want desperately to tell you how grateful I am that I have seen it.

One February, when I was visiting Ronco in southern Switzerland, I took a walk through the gray mist along the path of the mountains. On the other side of the lake, edged by cold fingers of ice, was another great stretch of the Alps. Along the ridge of the heights beyond me, the snow lay like a lace shawl. On that side the sun suddenly broke through the clouds and the mountains clapped their hands with joy. I stood still, to savor the moment. If Cezanne had painted the scene and given me the canvas to hang on the wall of my library, I could not remember it more vividly.

Seeing your soul as it approaches the *mysterium tremendum* is like the transporting wonder of that moment at Ronco. You would rebuke me severely for those words, and dismiss what I am about to say, so perhaps it is just as well that these words are restricted to my tablet.

How did you become the person you are? Your heritage is a noble one. In this minute, I can see the black border and the dark print of that formal announcement of your father's death, and, later on, of your mother's. I remember that tall, stately town house in which your father lived and practiced medicine for so long. I can see his face, so strikingly similar to his colleague Carl Jung: the white hair and mustache, the high dome of his forehead, broad shoulders. I can also see your mother's patrician face, her bent figure, and her

graceful style combining dignity and humility as only people
of her generation and privilege could do. Nor do I forget
that you are one of eight children, each of whom rose to the
top of his career—two in medicine, three in business—to say
nothing of the distinction of your sisters and their fortunate
marriages.

Doubtless, all of that background formed the crucible in
which your soul was shaped, but you were the one who was
doing the shaping. How did it happen? What is the key? I
long to understand the riddle of how you became
Raymond? How did you escape the snare of considerable
wealth? How did you manage to slip out of the noose of
material preoccupations when so many of your counterparts
in the corporate business community hang themselves by it?
Why did you live in a modest, rented two-bedroom
apartment for thirty years, when you could have bought a
house of grandeur and beauty anywhere? And when you
built your dream house in the Berkshires, why did you build
a dwelling of such utter simplicity that it is almost
indistinguishable from the meadow in which it sits? Oh, I
know you built a guest cottage and other buildings on the
property. I have not forgotten how you acquired hundreds
of acres and enjoyed the life of your farm in the good hands
of two treasured friends over the years. Yet, when I look at
the material side of your life history, the scale is invariably
simple, unpretentious, and the style is elegant, pure,
unique. How did you keep it that way? Why did the siren
of success never lure you from your essentiality?

Some might tell me that your Calvinist puritanism
blocked you from the love of ease, but that is fatuous, easy
palaver. The answer is far deeper than the social and

psychological mores of the bourgeoisie in the early part of this century.

The key is somewhere in the realm of the moral-spiritual sphere. I regret that we talked so little about your boyhood, because I am convinced that an event or a series of events of primal importance happened to you in early manhood or late adolescence, which caused you to make a profound commitment of yourself and your future. I believe it was a commitment to truth, inward truth and outward truth—something like Shakespeare's dictum "To thine own self be true." That commitment, made in an early moment of illumination, became the polestar of your journey. It is the radiance of that experience that has kept you humble in spite of all your successes and honors. Without that steadfast loyalty to the knowledge of your own truth and the truth you insisted upon in your relations with everyone who came across your path, you would never have become the Raymond I know. It is from that habit of mind and spirit that there was formed in you a core of moral strength of such intensity that I know of no one in your business career or in your personal life who ever had the faintest doubt about your integrity. It was not something you ever mentioned, nor did it ever make you self-righteous. You were too aware of your inner struggles and responsibilities to assume any moral superiority over anyone.

Was that inward consciousness the source of your reserve? Whatever it was, your trustworthiness made you the safe bearer of many secrets. We who know you know that any secret information about ourselves that we entrusted to you is as secure in your keeping as though we had never shared it with anyone; for we knew that your moral sensitivity would regard a breach of trust as the betrayal of the core of your being.

The simplicity of your life, your freedom from the power of possessions, your ability to put material success in its proper place, your consistent practice of responsible stewardship for the benefit of others, your abiding integrity and trustworthiness, your moral stamina, all this and more have formed a soul that is abundantly ready for the mystery of the next world.

There is, however, one remaining province of elementary importance in the formation of the soul, which you have dealt with in your own special way. It is the province of the spirit. Religion has been a central fact of your existence and the institutions of organized religion have benefitted from your generosity. Yet you have remained remarkably free of any taint of dogmatism or excessive zeal to impose your religious views on others. Like your life, you have kept your religion simple, elementary. I know you believe in the reality of the spiritual world. Prayer, quiet reflective prayer, is a part of how you have lived your daily life. God is the breath of your life, and I don't believe you have ever doubted that mystery. The deepest note in this sphere of experience for you, though, is the Christ Event. Your whole character is rooted in that event more deeply than you or I or anyone will ever know. It is where the river of your life had its beginning, and it is in the ocean of that mystery where it will have its ending.

The unusual quality I see in your religious roots is tentativeness. When it comes to the questions of faith and life's ultimate meaning, there is always a whisper in you that says "I'm not quite sure." It is not a voice so strident or self-important that it prevents you from persevering and practicing the things of spiritual awareness. Nor is it so soft that you seldom hear it. I think it is a whisper you have determinedly learned to live with. It is a paradox. It is that very borderline between certainty and uncertainty on which you have walked so many years, which makes you inordinately dear to the heart of God.

As you well know, none of us lives as an island. The bridge between you and over fifty years of your life history is Lydia, It is no accident that the woman you chose to marry was a person who could blow with the breath of her profound devotion and love on the embers of your soul, and rekindle again and again the glow of your dedication to truth and responsibility, freedom and simplicity, as well as spiritual sensitivity. Her gifts of the soul are not unlike your own, but with Lydia there was never any need for severe determination or excessive willpower. Nor did she have to struggle with the nagging whisper of doubt or the ethical problems of choice and judgment in a host of complex situations. All she needed was her love of you, your love of her, and the handiwork of God's good earth around her. Moral clarity, trustworthiness, freedom from power and possessions, the reality of God, the abyss of light we call Christ, are all as real and natural to Lydia as the breast of a mother's milk is to her child. She was born that way, and the love between you and Lydia has kept her that way.

There is a photo of her that is before me now on my desk. She is wearing a brown cardigan sweater buttoned to the top. A pink and white kerchief is tucked around her neck and softly folded beneath the sweater. Her strong, lined face with that straightforward look of hers, free of shame and fear, fixes me in rapt attention. She is asking me a question and she knows she will receive the truth. Oh, Raymond, how blessed you have been all these years by Lydia! Your soul would not be as ready for the next sphere as it is, had it not been for Lydia.

I think of her gardens. The flowing shapes, the profusion of color so carefully planned and planted, the stone wall you built together, and it suddenly comes over me that all the beauty, the prodigious work of her hands, is but a symbol of the beauty and love Lydia gave to you, year after year after year.

Of course, I do not know when the call will come to move from this mortal house to the many-mansioned kingdom, but one thing I do know: your soul is ready, and so is Lydia's! There are no bondages to hold you back when you get there. You were never caught in the cul-de-sac of material preoccupation. You kept your souls close to the refining fires of truth. You had no question about the sovereign importance of responsibility for our behavior. You have remained as little children in the kingdom of God, standing with sand pails before the ocean of divine majesty and mystery. You and Lydia are two souls who will never be separated. You will go from strength to strength, from glory to glory.

As ever,

Dear Lydia,

Every day I think of you and the ceaseless routine of your care of Raymond. I see you quick-stepping your way over the short distance from your apartment to Raymond's room in the extended care facility where he waits for your morning arrival. I can see his finely drawn face, which I never tire of admiring. His mouth is tightly closed like a blade snapped shut in a knife. His blind eyes are squeezed shut as he pursues the trail of blazing fires in the confusing forest of his memory. His restless hands fumble at the buttons of his shirt. The whiteness of his hair is so pure it almost reflects the rays of the morning sun.

You come into his room with your words of endearment and tenderness. He greets you with a minimum of words. A few minutes pass, and presently he is lost in his own world again. Sometimes it is a hideous and fearful world from which he is desperate to escape, but most of the time he is preoccupied with the effort to endure what must be endured and to control his rage against the indignity of his all-encompassing helplessness.

Occasionally there comes a clearing in the woods. The

demons of confusion and anger leave him. His responses are positive. Inner peace enfolds both of you. A period of acceptance makes life bearable. Some mornings you find him in this condition but, alas, by afternoon it is gone and the old desperate short-fused irritability is back again. Silence prevails until the blessed escape of sleep spreads her mantle in the room once more.

Lydia, my dear, I have often said to myself, how could it be otherwise? When a person of character and lifelong strength is shorn of every dignity, no longer able to see, incontinent, weakened by strokes that rob him of mobility and every freedom, unable to sustain a thought beyond three or four minutes, barely capable of a few shuffling steps from his bed to his chair, having to be fed his meals and bathed as though he were an infant, why shouldn't he be outraged by his fate? I am not surprised that he doesn't welcome old friends. Their good fortune and vigorous health must seem monstrous compared to his own condition. The contrast can only exacerbate his rage against the falling of the light.

Indeed I confess, Lydia, that I find Raymond's barely repressed anger, his prolonged silences, his withdrawn presence, eminently worthy of my respect. There is something noble about it. When the slings and arrows of outrageous fortune find their target in a helpless victim, you cannot fail to admire the victim when he refuses to bow his head before his fate. Isn't that far better than abject passivity?

You and I know there is a way between passivity and resistance by which we can meet the defeats and disappointments of life, but I'm not sure we would recognize it if our minds couldn't see it. If every day was a battle with helplessness, compelling us to be dependent on someone else all the way from cleaning up our own excrement to changing our clothes for sleep at night, I suspect our only choices would be either to fight it or to acquiesce. I would hope I would have enough strength of character to claim my humanity to the end by refusing to become a victim in the hands of my caretakers. When I saw Raymond put up his fists like a boy on the school playground and strike out at the nurses as they started to prepare him for his bath, I smiled with deep encouragement. "Let 'em have it, Ray," I said to myself.

When I step back, my dear Lydia, and think about this long, slow steady decline toward death, I can only pray and plead, "Release him, blessed Saviour, release him. Take him unto thyself. Deliver him from the bondage of this flesh. Bring him into the kingdom of everlasting light."

Doubtless that is a prayer your mind acknowledges, but which your heart denies. Wisdom tells you that you do not want Raymond to continue this "living death." Yet your life has had its entire focus on him in such total love and devotion that you cannot help feeling that as long as you can have him with you, no matter what his condition, you are happier than you would be without him. To have even a few occasional fleeting moments of exchange and tenderness make all the sacrifice and effort worthwhile to you.

No one will ever know what you have experienced day and night for the past three years. You have watched Raymond slip away from you inch by inch. His anger today is like a steady background buzzing in the atmosphere. What it must have been like when he first became aware of his inability to think and to act with his customary command and éclat, I tremble to think.

Few of us adjust to major frustrations gracefully. Those who have never suffered fools gladly are not likely to suffer incapacities in themselves very well.

Obviously, the person who has to live with the snap and bark of a beloved spouse coping with decreasing energies is likely to become the object of irrational abuse and irritation. Who can handle unwarranted accusations and projections of blame with a serene and quiet mind? Unjustified criticism always stings, but it never stings so hurtfully as it does when it comes from someone we love. Our rational mind tells us that these ministrokes, which rob the brain of its blood supply, are responsible for these outbursts of cruel attack. We tell ourselves not to take them personally! But we do! We can't help it. Feelings are feelings, and it doesn't help matters to pretend that we are untouched by sharp words and conscious unkindness.

It would never be your method of defense, Lydia, because you are too honest. However, I have seen a husband or a wife react to the verbal abuse of their afflicted spouses by treating them as though they were little children: "There, there, my dear, I know you don't mean what you say and we mustn't talk that way any more!" I must confess that when I have seen the reaction of anger such treatment releases, I have enjoyed it. (One man I saw threw his bedside clock at his wife!) To speak to any human beings above the age of three as though they were infants is unconscionable in my book.

Is it not far better to react to unfair anger, even from a spouse who cannot be wholly responsible for his behavior, by plainly revealing our own hurt and openly withdrawing from the scene until the weather has changed? I like the honesty of that strategy, and who knows, perhaps it helps to introduce some measure of control into the situation.

Unpredictability is at the core of this misery. Before Raymond reached his present point of no return, life was a constant flow of bewilderment. You never knew what mood he might be in on any given day. Sometimes it was like sailing before a fair wind. The sky was unclouded, filled with the warmth of a summer sun. Reason was in charge of the tiller, but the very next day life was unmitigated hell again. On the sun filled days you couldn't help it if you kept saying to yourself, "Oh, if only it would last." Sometimes it did, and sometimes it didn't.

It is hard for me to find even a grain of comfort in Raymond's present condition, but I suppose there is bound to be some relief in not being tied any longer to the extremes of hope and despair. Now we accept the fact that the most we can hope for is to have a few minutes in a day when the sky clears and the shadows flee away.

Last night the moonlight cast its magic spell over our landscape. I sat on the steps of my study, captured by the strangeness of the scene. The ocean was as tame as a lamb. Though it is only a few hundred yards across the marsh pond and the sand dunes to the lip of the sea, I could barely hear the rhythm of its breathing power. Once or twice I heard the rapid sucking of thousands of pebbles and stones being drawn out to sea as the ocean inhaled, but otherwise silence prevailed. A southwesterly wind danced among the trees. The white surface of the pond lay passive and naked before the gaze of the moon. The shrubbery and a cedar tree at the edge of the water played tricks with my imagination. I was certain someone was crouching at the foot of the hill. Now he was at one place, now at another. Several of us have been burglarized. Who *was* that down there? With flashlight in hand, I crept near to the area that had fixed my attention. Then I switched the flashlight on and focused the beam on the suspicious spot. It was a sumac bush bending before the breeze.

Lydia, I wonder if the landscape of last night's experience is not like the landscape of Raymond's mind? As I read over what I have written in this letter to you, it occurs to me this morning that I have dwelt too long on Raymond's resistance and resentment in his present straitjacket. Perhaps the truth is that most of the time Raymond's consciousness is like my own last night. Everything is bathed in a strange and threatening light. Nothing is quite real, save the projections of our own fears and phantoms. Unexpected details catch our attention and we become fixed with a notion that something is what it is not. Then the fever passes until a new restlessness seizes us. Sleep then becomes a blessed relief.

So, my dear, enough about Raymond. Some simple thoughts have come to me that I hope you might find helpful for your use in handling the constant drain on your energies these days.

My first thought comes from my own experience in prolonged care of persons in Raymond's condition. It was a friend, now dead. As I look back on that friendship I have every reason to believe that nothing ever troubled the depths of our devotion to one another. Yet there was one day when I was feeding him his lunch and he knocked the spoon from my hand and angrily said, "Get away from me. I don't want you to touch me." I managed to recoup my forces enough to finish the lunch and coax him to bed for his afternoon nap. When I left the nursing home, I could not deny my hurt. I felt misused, insulted, rejected. I couldn't escape the feeling that he knew what he was doing and that he deliberately chose to hurt me. It was several hours before I came to my senses and realized that it was a temporary tempest, which I was sure he wouldn't even remember after his midday siesta.

There are, Lydia, I'm sure, times when you must experience similar reactions to Raymond's outbursts, or to his silences. Don't deny them. They are the natural reactions of any human being in such circumstances. It may help to write about your hurt. When you offer love and have it thrown back at you, the sting can be intolerable, but, remember, with Raymond it is only a sting. It is an accident of the moment. You happened to get in the way at the wrong time. It is almost immediately forgotten.

Your task is to put it in perspective as soon as possible and forget it also. Please don't blame yourself for the hurt. There was nothing you could have done to have anticipated it or to have prevented it. Give the whole incident to the mercy of God, and recall one of the many golden times when you and Raymond were lyrically close to one another. Then dwell on it awhile with praise and thanksgiving. The warmth of the memory will heal the hurt.

Above all, Lydia, keep a weather eye on the storms of guilt. They can cloud the horizon so disastrously that you lose your way entirely. You may say to yourself, "If only I could spend more time with him, he would improve," or

"If only I could reach him with more love and kindness, maybe he would feel better about his limitations," or "If only my faith were stronger and if my prayers were more constant, God would heal him," or "Perhaps I should never have moved him from our home to this nursing facility," or "Perhaps he would respond to someone who is not so emotionally bound up to him as I am. Maybe I'm not the right person to be taking care of him now," or "I should have recognized the serious nature of his problems earlier than I did. If I had done so, things might be different today," or "I wonder if we shouldn't have changed doctors several years ago. Perhaps I should have taken him to a place like the Mayo Clinic when all this began," or "I wonder if I should have been more aggressive in persuading him to have obtained treatment for our problem long ago," or "I wonder if he was as happy with me all these years as I thought he was."

Guilty thoughts of that character are endless. They are moles that undermine our love and leave us vulnerable to irrational devastation. They rob us of joy. We are reduced to such a point of vulnerability that we can't enjoy even an evening with friends, a concert, the theater, or a happy meal with a treasured sister, because we think it is neither right nor fair for us to be enjoying something denied our spouse.

Such devastation has to stop, or it could take us to the grave before our slowly dying spouse even approaches it. I can hear you saying to me, "But how do I stop it?" The clue is detachment.

Many years ago, I remember phoning you when you and Raymond were away. A fire had damaged your home. I was present as the fire was being brought under control. The fire chief asked how we could be in touch with you. I was the only one present who knew how to reach you. The person who answered the phone said you were not available but she would get a message to you. I told her to tell you there had been a fire at your home and to ask you to call me. Fortunately, although the fire was damaging, it was not as extensive as we had feared.

The thing I shall always remember about that fire was something you said to me a week later. You told me that after you received the message you had to walk some little distance to the nearest phone to return my call. Then you added, "The amazing thing to me was I realized that, although there were many things at home which I treasured, none of them mattered in any real sense to me. After all, they were just things: furniture, rugs, china, silver, art objects, and paintings. None of them owned me. I owned them and could let them go if I had to do so."

I have cherished that memory, my dear, because it told me much about the authentic depth of your spirit. Not many of us are capable of freedom and detachment in a moment of loss.

Those depths need to be called upon now. You have a rare pearl of the spirit. There is not an ounce of avariciousness or covetousness in you. Jealousy is an emotion that you have only heard of. You know neither its twistedness nor its subtlety because clutchy possessiveness is not in your nature. By a blessed grace you have preserved a childlike spirit of extraordinary freedom. It is an interior humility of the heart, which makes you abundantly available to a host of friends, learned and ignorant, rich and poor, wise and foolish.

My prayer these days is that these qualities of the soul may now come to your aid as you cope with the need to detach yourself from the one unconditional attachment of your life, which is your unceasing devotion to Raymond. There is nothing anyone could ask you to do that could be as painful and difficult as that which you are now required to undertake. Had your life for half a century not found its polestar in Raymond, the task would not be filled with so much anguish. However, that's the way it is, Lydia, and neither you nor I would wish it were different. The world seldom sees such absolute devotion and faithfulness. All of us who have known you both have been blessed by the knowledge of your unlimited love for Raymond and his love for you. Yet now neither of us can deny the law of change. Things are not as they used to be. The current of your love for Raymond is as steadfast and strong as it ever was. At the subterranean level of the riverbed, Raymond's love for you is as constant and profound as it ever was, but there is almost no way for you to know it. The river seems almost stagnant, save for an occasional squeezing of the hand, or when he rests his head on your shoulder. The absence of mutuality, the cessation of communication, compels a change of the relationship. You no longer have a partner, but a patient. I well know that an effort of Herculean proportions is required of you if you are to adjust to this reality, but, my dear, you have no choice if you are to survive. The time has come when you must find the courage to apply that gift of detachment and childlike freedom to your attachment to Raymond. You must begin to think of your marriage as something that was rounded out somewhere near your golden anniversary. Offer God many flowers of praise and gratitude for the length and breadth and depth of all you shared with Raymond. Cultivate as much circumspection as you can, and join me in praying for Raymond's release from the bondage of this flesh. Let no urgency or tension come into your prayers. Step back and whisper to yourself, ''What will be, shall be.'' Surrender the future to the mysterious workings of destiny.

And then, dear Lydia, get out! Do things. Entertain and be entertained. You enjoy people of all ages and walks of life. Fill your days with as much richness and pleasure as you can comfortably handle. Don't allow the demon of guilt to dictate your daily routines. Raymond may resist your absences for an afternoon, a weekend, a holiday, an evening; but there are other people to fill the vacuum, and you are soon back again. He can adjust to that. When he asks one of us who cares for him in your absence ''Where's Lydia?'' you can be confident that we will provide abundant reassurance, and in a few moments he will have forgotten the question.

In short, Lydia, I am begging you to affirm your own right to life. Just because Raymond's life is ebbing is no reason for yours to do the same. There is much that remains for you to do. God is asking you to assume the responsibility of being the steward of your time and resources for the purposes he has put in your heart. The future has new duties and new joys awaiting you.

I need not dwell for any length on the inward dimensions of this strange new chapter in your life story. You have a natural and well-established pattern of quietness and solitude. Cultivate your secret garden. Enrich the soil of it by much trustfulness in the love of God. By-and-by you will reap a blessed harvest of serenity and peace.

I remember, years ago, exploring underground caverns in Virginia. When we drew near the exit, the guide told us to extinguish our flashlights. As soon as we did so, we could see a faint radiance that grew brighter and brighter every few feet until we emerged in the daylight. Sometimes, Lydia, in the journey of the soul God asks us to become wholly dependent on him. The light of our own making is no longer useful. If we surrender even the most precious and beloved light we have, a wondrous thing happens. Behold, there is enough Godlight to guide us through the darkness. We might even have missed the exit if we hadn't put out our candles.

Do let me hear from you soon.

Much love,

Joe

My dear Son,

I wonder what you thought as you sealed your recent letter? Was your heart heavy with foreboding about its effect on me? Did some voice say, "Well, now, I've put the issues on the table," or were you simply reaching out to redefine our relationship? I suppose your prevailing mood at the time was a little of each and more, much more, than I have mentioned. Believe me, I desire nothing so intensely as a redefinition of our relationship in a way that is mutually real and open and satisfying. My soul cries out for it. Obviously, I cannot accomplish it alone, nor can you; but please trust me when I say that I am prepared to give it whatever time and energy it may require.

There is much in what you say that is valid. I want to clarify the validity of your observations from my perspective. However, before I do that, please indulge me in two minor reflections.

I was surprised to learn that you walked away from our meeting shaking your head in disbelief as you approached the elevators in your building. I thought we had begun a discussion that held much promise for the future. As we crossed Sixth Avenue heading for the Time-Life Building, we were deep into one of our favorite subjects, having to do with politics, the present administration, issues of social justice; and it felt like old times to me. I had a midafternoon appointment for which I was a trifle late. As I sat in the cab going uptown, I was nothing but thankful for our time together.

My perception of the time factor in our luncheon was also different from your own. We were together a little over two hours. It was almost 2:30 when we got back to your office. If I seemed to terminate our visit precipitously, perhaps it was because I assumed you had to get back to work, and I'm sure I was conscious of my next commitment.

Now to the valid observations of your letter. Yes, I agree that the word "script" was an ill-chosen and badly motivated description of our past differences. However, I do not agree that my use of the term was evidence of unexpressed hostility toward you. My dreams are full of you. When I read my journals I find you and Tim and Peter appear in my sleep consciousness with amazing regularity. There appears to be no regular pattern. Sometimes the three of you are very small. We are engaged in some game in our Swarthmore house, or we are pushing ourselves through crowds in Harvard Square. At other times it is just the two of us. You are your present age, and we are frequently engaged in a dialogue about the craft of writing, about which we both have insuperable problems. I have no record of a dream in which, either covertly or overtly, we are caught in a cross fire of hostility. Throughout your growing life you were an unmitigated satisfaction to me.

Doubtless that has something to do with the joy that seems to accompany my dreams of you. Nor could I ever use the word "hostile" to describe my feelings about you in my present consciousness.

Nevertheless, you were justified in reacting to the word "script." When I asked you to tell me how and why we had fallen out of touch with each other in the past year, you mentioned your unreadiness for my remarriage only fourteen months after your mother's death. You referred to your brother's death and how you felt the burden of fulfillment in my progeny fell heavily on your shoulders after he was gone. You said our house in Rhode Island had become almost a ghost-filled place for you and that you slept badly when you were here. These were things you have mentioned to me in previous conversations. That, however, did not justify the implication that such feelings belonged to the category of old tapes, and for that I beg your forgiveness. Indeed, repetition should have alerted me to the depth and complexity of your feelings, eliciting my most careful attention and reflection. I am sorry for my insensitivity.

Now as to your observation regarding your mother's goading the truth out of me. That is quite an accurate way to put it! She did it often, and she would not let me off the hook until the fish was landed. I have long recognized that I am one of those persons who prefers peace at any price. My needs for love are gargantuan. I will do almost anything rather than threaten their fulfillment. Can you understand, dear man, how grateful I am to your mother for that demand of truth in her?

You may think the characteristic of evasion to which

your letter refers is static, but that is far from the case. Your mother needed what I brought to her as much as I needed what she brought to me, but I surely needed her astringency. I needed to be challenged to produce the depth of my feelings. I needed to deal with negatives and evasions. I needed to change those patterns of defense. I needed to stop withdrawing and to confront the real scope of a problem as honestly and clearly as possible. I needed to learn that running away from a problem or repressing it never solves it. She taught me all of that. My experience in therapy had revealed the pattern to me, but it was through living with her that I learned to change it. If you think my responses to you are evidence that I have not learned how to be genuinely present to another in the face of conflict, then I beg you to try me, as one adult to another. ''You'll like it,'' as the commercial says, and so will I!

Yes, I did think you had some unresolved ''work'' to do regarding your mother's death. I would not call it ''obsessive.'' That is not the way I have thought about it at all. You were almost twenty when she died. At fifteen you went to Groton, then came Harvard. Those six or seven years were years of resolution for your mother and me. We had achieved an incomparable openness and, in spite of all the complications of her cancer, it was, I am sure, her victory, not mine. However, I never denied the validity of our undertaking or the crucial importance of it. I knew my soul's survival depended on it. In the last two years of her life there was a profound peace that largely prevailed between us. Many people remarked on it. It was a closing of the circle. We were back at the point of mutuality, trust, and openness where we had begun thirty-two years previously. When she died it was that sense of closure that set me free to go on with life. My only reason for touching on this development, beloved man, is that it is something you had little opportunity to observe because you were not there.

After her death, I tried several times to explore with you what you were feeling. Friends would ask me, "How is your son taking his mother's death?" I would answer, "I really don't know. He is clearly going on with his life quite happily, but I don't know how he is handling his grief since he doesn't feel free to talk about it." I hope that wasn't my fault. I did try to bring up the subject repeatedly. However, I suppose you were "not surprisingly" using your father's pattern of defense by simply pushing the hurt and emptiness out of your consciousness.

The unanswered question in my mind is how you have accommodated your mother's anger in your psyche. If my dominant negative behavior in the family constellation of emotional patterns was escape, hers was anger. For twenty-six of our thirty-two years of marriage, her unpredictable irritability and uncontrollable rages marked all of us. Her sisters avoided her company because of it. Her mother was denied her presence in the last decade of her life because of it. My mother stopped visiting us because of it. There was no evidence of excessive rage in her relations to her family, nor to me, nor to my family, until Holly was born. From then until two years before her death, not a day went by without some occasion of intense irritability, if not outright anger. Her prolonged experience of therapy never adequately explained it to me. Perhaps it did to her. I don't know. I am sure I contributed substantially to the problem, but in spite of my proclivities to guilt I have come to the firm conclusion that I was not responsible for it. One of the things that has saved me in this painful remembrance is that I recall how she often said to me with characteristic integrity and compassion, "Don't blame yourself. It's not your fault."

You were the child she enjoyed more than any of your siblings. You were at the end of the line and she ached to enjoy your infancy as she had not been able to do previously. Unquestionably there were satisfactions, but you also came in for your share of her negative energies. I wonder how you have integrated the shadow side of your relation to your mother.

Lord knows, there was an abundance on the bright side—her integrity, her standards of taste, intellect, spiritual authenticity, and her insistence upon respect and honor in our personal relationships, above popularity and accommodation. It is impossible for any of us in the family to conceive what the furniture of our minds would be like without the constant supply of books and ideas with which she furnished us. Nor would our judgments about things and people be what they are without the model of her life. Our debt of gratitude for her is beyond measure. I know you feel this as deeply as I do.

You refer in this letter to a tendency in me to manipulate the responses of those who are close to me. You kindly do not use the word "manipulate," but I think that is what it is, and I try hard not to be guilty of that phenomenon. I recognize it in myself and I believe people dear to me have suffered because of it. You write, "Sometimes really being with someone (not as a counselor or a therapist or a pastor or a helper, but with your emotions on the line just as theirs are) really feels like a gigantic nuisance. I don't want to be made to feel, to hurt, or even to be joyful."

Maybe some of this tendency in me is a "father knows best" syndrome, and I am not so hard on myself as to think that my motivation at bottom is the need for power over others. I think you will agree that my desire is one of serving the best interest of those I love. Yet you are quite right. I don't welcome being made to feel something or to do something, however well intentioned it may be, that I have not come to wish of my own accord and out of my own free will. Why should I think others would feel differently?

You touch a nerve that is oversensitive. My family, my sisters and brothers, all have had to deal with what I call "the Bishop Control Syndrome." It has to do with our father's death, our early economic insecurities, our family anxieties, and the determination among each of us to control our destinies in such a way as to protect ourselves against the arrows of outrageous fate. We are all of us in varying degrees smitten with the excessive control bug.

In my case a traumatic experience following my service as a navy chaplain in World War II contributed significantly to the syndrome. A shock reaction seized me after I was mustered out of the navy. I couldn't function. I couldn't make house calls or preach or concentrate, except with the most intense concentration. I withdrew. The loss of control was a nightmare I'll never forget. Therapy, prayer, the love of friends, restored me, but the fear of a repeat never left me. Some measure of my tendency to manipulate surely arises from that experience.

I ask you now to trust that I recognize this tendency in myself with anguish. It grieves me when I see myself behaving this way. I have, through Peggy's love of me, come to see the scandalous persistence of that form of behavior. It is a far better expression of love to step back sometimes, than it is to step forward. If I have been too forward-putting in my love for you, please forgive me, and let's try again. Gently, lovingly, call me on it, and together we'll change it.

Did I express myself so poorly in my last letter as to imply that if I am patient, as you say, you will go the same route as your brother and sister have gone in resolving their relations to me? Did I indicate that if you could "attain the same level of maturity" apparently achieved by your brother and sister, "our relationship would be magically mended"? Such a conclusion is unconscionable. If I implied it, I wholeheartedly apologize for it and reject it. To be sure, each of you is a person. I cannot compare you in any degree. I do not expect that your journeys should be similar. Holly is a great joy and support to me these days. Tim and I have a loving and mutually accepting relation in spite of our profound differences over questions of biblical interpretation and the character of the Christian faith. If I mentioned both of these truths in a way that seemed to compare unfavorably to our relation, please forgive me. They are not comparable, and I fully recognize that you and I have a different road to travel to our destination; but the destination is the same for all three relations, namely, a destiny of mutual respect and love.

This brings me to the last point in your letter. You write, "Finally, and most crucially, there is the matter of love and it is here that I feel the greatest pain. I assure you I don't have the slightest problem in affirming my love for you. I love you deeply. I always have and I always will. I, too, have hundreds—no, thousands—of fond memories about my childhood with you—in so many ways you were an absolutely wonderful father. My feelings about that will never change. But for some reason you have always behaved as if love should preclude conflict, as if love should make the way smooth and effortlessly remove the rocks of life. Of course you know that's not true in your head, but in your heart I think you believe it. My love for you not only does not preclude conflict, it positively demands it.''

Thank you, dear man, for that affirmation of love of me. I need not repeat the depth of my unyielding love for you, except to say that this honest letter of yours only confirms again my commitment to you.

I wish I could say you are mistaken about my problem regarding conflict and love, but you are more right than even you could know. As I have already said, conflict is not my natural way. The early deprivation of love in my fatherless life was too raw for me to risk the loss of love from any quarter that gave it to me. It has ever been thus with me.

You say that I am arbitrary, that I withdraw precipitously from a conflictual discussion between us, leaving you ''gasping for breath, wondering if [I] was ever really present'' with you in your effort to share important feeling or reflection. I don't remember such occasions, but I have no doubt that they occurred. I am quite adroit in forgetting what I want to forget.

With the years I have become comfortable with conflict

in my professional life. My future does not depend on acceptance or on popularity. I don't ask to be loved, but to be respected. I work hard to understand my positions on issues, and I don't feel required to defend those positions but to state them quietly and with relaxed confidence that if I am mistaken the truth will show me my flaw. I am always on the side of truth, even when it is against me. There is no other position to take on which real security can be built. Conflict is a necessity in the pursuit of truth. Like you, I welcome it.

However, when it comes to personal relationships, conflict becomes more than a rational process. If I love someone, conflict is indeed difficult for me. I am threatened by it. I cannot help feeling this way. Some of my fear of it comes from my deep-seated sadness when I reflect on the damage your mother's need for conflict imposed on our marriage. As I have said, I know I would not have grown as much as I have, had she not engaged me in conflict. Nevertheless, there was much of it that was unnecessary, and the scars it left behind were often long in healing. I think we enter into the arena of conflict with someone dear to us at considerable peril to the outcome. Bare knuckles can leave us so bruised and guilty that we never want to make the attempt again.

I suppose it depends on the style with which we confront our differences together, does it not? For me, confrontation is fruitful and blessed when we speak the truth in love, gently, humbly, ever prepared to articulate our role in the problem and our contribution to the misunderstanding or to the hurt. As soon as moralism and judgments come into the discussion, the contest becomes clouded by feelings of guilt and righteousness, and before you know it, the hope of reconciliation is lost. Some people pull that one off with great results. I'm afraid I am not one of them. Some things I can change in myself, even in my old age, but that reaction of mine to negative confrontational tactics is not one of them. I really believe, though, when it is said with love and humility I can accept anything a dear one may say to me, together sifting the chaff from the wheat.

Your letter leads me to believe we can do that together. I welcome it! Moreover, I yearn for it, not only because I long to recover the joy and the fun of our old companionship sharing the dozen commonalities we both enjoy, but because my soul thirsts for it.

You see, I am at a stage in life when time seems beyond all price. I want to make as positive a use of my late years as I can. Above all, for my soul's sake I want to be reconciled and at peace with all the people who have been crucial in my journey. You must know, dear man, that you are very near the top of the list!

Hope to see you soon. I read your pieces in the magazine with avid interest. I pray your full and active life isn't too draining of your energies.

With much love,

Dad

My dearly beloved Sister,

Gratitude is an emotion that rises in me as regularly as the tide. I often walk down to the breach through which the ocean surges into our pond every night and day. The times that most fascinate me are those when the current at the mouth of the breach seems in conflict with itself. The flow is neither inward toward the pond nor outward to the ocean. It moves uncertainly one way, then another, equally caught between high and low tide.

Presently the decision is made, and while you have turned your head to speak to someone, the sweep of the ocean has taken over. The water rushes in, breaking on the rocks in abandoned victory. Within half an hour the power of the ocean current is so great you dare not sail against it.

As I sit here writing to you, the flow of my gratitude for all you have meant to my life since I was born is like the incoming tide. It rises out of an abundant depth. I am fairly overwhelmed by it. I ask myself, "Whence comes this stream?" Is it induced by the knowledge of your precarious health? No, "Old Thing," I'm sure that can't be true. Yet, perhaps a small portion of my intensity of feeling about you these days arises out of my fear of losing you. There is nothing like a life-threatening condition to put our values straight.

When I was a child, you were always there. Nine years difference in age doesn't seem like very much now, but to a two year old it was the difference between a child's world and a grown-up world. Do you remember my tricycle? I was king of the block riding around Phillips's seed store to greet the customers and to show them how fast I could go. You were sixteen or seventeen. I was six or seven.

I was devastated when a wheel was broken. That evening you produced one of your boyfriends, who brought a new cotter pin and fixed it. You were as happy to see me riding out of sight as I was to be going again. In the summer, can you forget how we used to catch lightning bugs together? Everyone else had their own mason jars in which to capture them, but you and I always shared a jar. I counted them and you caught them. I called them lightning bugs and you called them fireflies. In the dark of the lawn you held the jar while I watched the mysterious creatures cast their radiance on your hands, on and off, on and off.

When I broke my leg you read to me. My favorite book at the time was *King Arthur and the Knights of the Round Table*. You read it so beautifully. You loved Guinevere; I lost my heart to Lancelot. The day Dr. Vars took off the cast we both stared at the tiny bone that joined my ankle to my knee. You burst out in tears at the sight. Dr. Vars laughed and assured us both that one leg would look like the other before Easter came. Since you had already begun to tease me about how stupid I was in finding Easter eggs, I guess the date could not have been very far distant.

Then my mind jumps across half a century of time to the year when you visited us in Rye at Christmastime. It was the Sunday when we were celebrating a special Christmas breakfast for the children and their families. The parish hall was wall-to-wall with people. Orange juice, coffee, breakfast cake, passed from family to family as we sat cross-legged on the floor. My darling stepdaughter Deborah had made life-sized puppets of the creatures of the twelve days of Christmas. The seventh and eighth grade children had been practicing the routine. It was a wonder-filled time. First the song was performed for us with the children's choir singing the parts. We all became children as we joined the singing the second time around, roaring with pleasure as the appropriate puppets appeared above the curtain, two turtle doves, three French hens, five golden rings, seven swans swimming, and on to the twelve pipers piping.

When it was over, I stood up to thank everyone and to greet the children. Your face was far at the back, but I saw you before anyone else in that great happy throng. It was shining with pleasure in the occasion and love for me. How do we thank someone for the faithful love of a lifetime? I shall not attempt another word.

Now to the business of your letter. I'm so conflicted, Old Thing, by the issue, I hardly know what to say. After that telephone call came four months ago I turned to Peggy and said, "Holy smoke, I'm not ready for this at all." I knew you weren't well, but the thought that you could be seriously ill was firmly barred from my mind. You have come through so many crises with flags unfurled and spirit unbowed, I assumed it would ever be thus, at least for the duration of my lifetime!

After all, it has been twenty-eight years since you stood up to cancer of the uterus, and shortly thereafter to cancer of the lung. You have functioned with astounding energy and drive on one lung ever since. The mastectomy you had just a year and a half ago, scared me to the bone, but you took that in such courageous stride I was certain you would lick this dread disease again. Your faith in the healing power of God and your history as a cooperative and trustful patient produced an unbeatable combination. I believe you're invincible, my sweet.

To be sure, I well remember a time when your flags drooped at levels well below half-mast. That was another bond that bound us to one another. We both lost sons in their late teens through accidents. We were, both of us, far from being invincible when that sorrow shattered our lives. Grief is a private kind of pain, but "when the silver cord was snapped and the golden bowl was broken" you and I knew what that meant for the other in our very flesh.

And now you are asking me to share in a momentous decision. As I have said, four months ago I was wholly unprepared for this crisis. When your son John told me abut the cardiac arrest that accompanied the problem of fluid in your lung and oxygen deprivation, I could have kissed him when he explained that he panicked on the spot and pled with the doctor to "do something, do something, don't let her die." The respirator brought you back, and oxygen keeps you alive today.

Dear and blessed Old Thing, we have all been given some priceless time since that day of John's panic. I am unabashedly grateful. I know you are. We all have time to get ready, but I wonder if I will ever be ready.

As usual, you are ahead of us. You have tried to introduce the subject in our conversations several times. You say to me, "I don't want to go through that valley again." I know you are talking about your heart failure and the long slow climb back to strength. I also know you are trying to raise the subject of "heroic" treatment, should the crisis arise again, but I chicken out and change the subject.

The next day you say to me, "I detest living this way. If I can't get out and be involved in my church, in the community, and in the lives of my friends, enjoying them and giving to them, I don't want to stick around if I can help it." I ignore the deeper question you are raising and focus on your value to all of us. I say, "Don't expect so much. You are precious to all of us just as you are. You are able to get around with that oxygen contraption. You give to us all the time. Now don't talk nonsense." The subject is closed.

Now at last you have me cornered. I can't skirt around the issue any longer. I have seen your weariness. I have wept privately over the memory of your labored breathing and pain-filled face. You have skewered me with your plea, "If I start to fail again, please let me go, and don't put me on a respirator. I want to make that clear to my doctor, but I don't want to tell him until I have the family back of me. Please help me. I do not want to live this way. I have made my peace with God, and I know as sure as I know anything that Christ's love waits for me."

Well, Old Thing, you have netted me. I can't escape it any longer. I know beyond a doubt that if the tables were reversed I would be making the same plea. It is only selfishness that has made me run from the issue. Four months ago I couldn't have said it, but I can say it now, "I support you all the way." Love, as we poor mortals know it, has an inescapably selfish side to it. You are so important to me, I cannot imagine what life would be like not to have you there for me when I need you. Yet I know that you will always be "there" for me, and so now we must let the matter rest.

Your dear strong John! I am so impressed by him. He came to an acceptance of your request before I did. Some of that is due, I suspect, to the fact that he has seen your daily struggle at closer range than I can obtain at this distance of over a thousand miles. It is, however, also due to his remarkable maturity and good judgment. You have a wonderful son in that man, my sweet.

I think also of Bonnie. I know it has been one of the great joys of your life to see how she has grown to become the loving person and the caring teacher she is today. Her devotion to you is boundless. She will have as much difficulty in accepting your plea to us as I did, but her love for you will lead the way, just as it has for me. Neither of us would want to prolong your misery a minute beyond your wishes, and, besides, we both know that you are always right anyway!

A big hug, my love,

As ever,

J.

Dear Bonnie,

Before the tumult and the shouting fade altogether, I want to tell you how unforgettably wonderful you have been, both before your mother's death and afterwards.

I shall always remember your enquiring blue eyes that day in the doctor's office. I held my breath as he told us your mother would die in a few days unless we used the respirator again. Then when he added in his dry matter-of-fact way that he would advise us to recommend the treatment to your mother even in her weakened condition, I felt we were both tottering on the edge of a precipice. I had no idea what you were going to say. All I knew was that the issue was in your hands at that moment. Your mother would have done anything for you. When you said, "Well, Joe, she has made the decision, hasn't she? And I guess we have to honor that, don't we?" I knew I was in the presence of a real person, Bonnie, and all I had to do was to follow your lead. Your gentle, loving spirit given to your mother after that hour in the doctor's office was incredibly strong and consistent. In one of my last moments with her, I said, "Your Bonnie is one exceptional and beautiful daughter, Old Thing." She smiled, nodded, and said, "Isn't she!"

Of course, Bonnie, I shall forever treasure those last moments of your mother's life with us. She just stopped breathing, didn't she? The three of us—you, John, and I—stood around her bed in the hospital, our eyes fixed on her face, but there it was, not a wrinkle moved. The end was upon us. I have shared such moments with many people, but this one was unique. As we embraced one another, holding your mother's hands, huddling about her head, I prayed as I have never prayed before. When we stood up and looked at her face will you ever forget the quiet expression of purest peace that came over her eyes? It was a benediction of love that held us enthralled in a wee glimpse of eternity.

And now comes the adjustment of life without her. In some ways I am glad that you have the task of coping with your father's problems. His enfeeblement and limitations have long indicated the wisdom of care in a good nursing home; but your mother always knew that would kill him, and so she bore it in season and out of season. I worry about what will become of him. His handicaps have made him mostly a prisoner of his room. Someone will have to be found to prepare meals for him and to clean up the house. After the funeral you mentioned that you are considering some renovation in order to provide living space for him on one floor. A wise plan, my dear. In our eighties, falls can be disastrous.

All of these busy business details serve a useful purpose, Bonnie. They muffle the beat and throb of grief's pain at the beginning. The weeping heart has a chance to adjust behind the preoccupation with lawyers, wills being probated, finances, insurance forms, property decisions, death certificates, bills, banks, clothing, personal memorabilia, presents to friends.

When that stage is over, don't be surprised if the sorrow

comes upon you like a thief in the night. It can't be avoided any longer. Bow your head, dear Bonnie. Take the loss as the irretrievable reality it is.

I'm sure you have countless letters, or memories of them, in your mother's own clear schoolteacher's handwriting, telling you how much she loved you and how grateful she was for you. Please don't exaggerate your regrets. You were wonderful to your mother. She always carried at least one of your letters in her purse. I'll bet you find dozens of them hidden in boxes in her bedroom.

You well know that your mother has been in my prayer life every day. She comes to my mind in flashes of intense feeling dozens of times. Some memory comes back to me or some conversation some vision of her frail figure and birdlike face rises to the surface of my mind, unbidden and startling. Without hesitation, I lift the moment into the sphere of prayer. Then I commit her to the Eternal.

There was one aspect of her character I want to explain to you as I see it. She was afflicted with a burden of anxiety she kept carefully repressed from general view. Once when she was with us a few days in Rye, I raised the issue. She quickly agreed that all her life she had battled against the fear that tragedy could strike and alter the whole course of her existence, as it had done when our father was killed in a train accident. Your brother Freddie's death increased that power of anxiety in her soul.

A demon of insecurity entered her deep consciousness at that time and she never altogether succeeded in mastering it. Her marriage was not the most successful one in the world. However, she refused to give up on it. A fraction of her perseverance was dictated by her fear of economic deprivation. The specter of poverty, real or unreal, was sufficient to arouse prodigious energies of protectiveness for the two of you as well as for herself.

Insecurity is the father of many offspring. It need not always be an unsightly and undesirable product. In your mother it produced a compulsion to control her environment and all the people in it. We all teased her about it in late life and she had the good grace to join in the laughter. She assumed she always knew best; in 80 percent of the time she did, wouldn't you agree? Her motives were never petty or malicious. I know of no instance in which she intended anything except the welfare and happiness of others. After a lifetime of controlling people around her, it became second nature to her.

A couple of years before her death we began talking about this pattern. She had no resistance to the truth about it. She was preoccupied with the happiness and growth of the large circle of friends in which she moved. Her capacity for love toward those blessed people was truly boundless. You have only to recall the grief so many people expressed at her funeral to see the authentic quality of her love for others. If the insecurities we all carry produced as much loving activity on behalf of others as they did in your mother, the earth would be a Garden of Eden again!

Now, Bonnie, isn't it a singular fact that someone of your mother's compulsions should be capable of releasing her grip on life as decisively as she did? It is quite unexpected, don't you think? One would anticipate a long hard bitter struggle to the end in such a person. Had I known only one side of your mother's nature, I would have predicted a battle for every inch of life, no matter how miserable it became. But she was the one who let go, and she was the one who persuaded us to let go.

Where did that freedom come from? I think it was partly her love of all of us that couldn't bear to see us suffer for her any more, but on a deeper plane I think that almost debonair liberty of spirit she had in her last best days arose from the depths of her faith. She knew in her bones she was a child of the Eternal and she knew her destiny was to inhabit a many-mansioned kingdom prepared for her by our Redeemer. I know she rested on that rock because that's the way we prayed together three days before she died.

So, precious Bonnie, your mother's soul is safely anchored in the haven of the eternal kingdom. Life has returned to life. Love has returned to love. Light has returned to light. Let your heart rest in that assurance and behold your darling mother going from glory to glory to glory.

Peace and love, my sweet,